THE DRAWINGS OF
WILLIAM HOGARTH
BY A·P·OPPÉ

PHAIDON

Wᵐ Hogarth

TERRACOTTA BUST BY LOUIS FRANÇOIS ROUBILIAC
ABOUT 1732
NATIONAL PORTRAIT GALLERY · LONDON

THE DRAWINGS OF
WILLIAM HOGARTH
BY A·P·OPPÉ

LONDON·MCMXLVIII

PHAIDON PRESS LTD

1948
PRINTED IN GREAT BRITAIN BY SUN PRINTERS LTD : WATFORD

PREFACE

Grateful acknowledgment *is due to H.M. The King for gracious permission to reproduce the fine series of drawings by Hogarth in the Royal Collection, and to the Marquess and Marchioness of Exeter for the facilities kindly afforded to study and reproduce the historic and almost unknown collection at Burghley House. Without these drawings, which were acquired by the ninth Earl of Exeter largely direct from Hogarth's widow, no publication could have any claim to represent Hogarth as a draughtsman. I am also indebted to the Trustees of the Pierpont Morgan Library, the New York Public Library and the British Museum for permission to reproduce the drawings in their collections. Of those who have helped me, I am especially grateful to Miss Felice Stampfle of the Pierpont Morgan Library whose detailed information has compensated for the lack of opportunity to examine the drawings themselves, to Mr. Croft Murray with whom I have discussed the drawings at the British Museum, and to Sir Owen Morshead and Miss Scott-Elliot who have enabled me to consult constantly the unrivalled collection of prints in the Royal Library. My thanks are also due to Dr. Antal, Mr. R. B. Beckett, Professor Joseph Burke and Mr. L. Goldscheider for the communication of information and publications and the loan of photographs, and to the Director of the National Gallery of Scotland and others for permission to examine their collections and for their forbearance when the results proved negative.*

The principal feature of this publication, the main series of plates, is confined to drawings which are either by Hogarth or have an old and hitherto unshaken claim to be so considered. Some others of equally good authority have been placed for convenience as illustrations in the text of the catalogue, where the more important among the drawings of which the attribution is doubtful are also reproduced. Drawings which are still missing and several which are held to be spurious are either described, with illustrations, in the appendix or are noticed where appropriate in the catalogue itself. The latter will be found by reference to the index. No oil sketches are included; they would have introduced a completely new series of problems which can be more properly treated in connection with Hogarth's paintings. Similarly, in the commentary, details of personal or topical interest have not, as a rule, been discussed since these belong to the prints rather than the drawings, and in some cases would have involved descriptions of prints for which there are no drawings. They have, moreover, been dealt with at length by the older commentators and are fully summarized in the British Museum Catalogue of Political and Personal Satires.

London : June 1948   *Paul Oppé*

CONTENTS

INTRODUCTION

IN the last quarter of the eighteenth century, the fashion for collecting Hogarth's engravings was at its highest. The prices paid by enthusiastic amateurs for early proofs and rare prints, however insignificant in themselves, were deplored as fantastic, and a collector who despaired of ever obtaining some outstanding rarity was lucky if he was allowed a tracing from the treasure of a more fortunate rival. Naturally, the enthusiasm extended to Hogarth's drawings. They did not command the same high prices in the sale-room, perhaps, as always, because, being unique, they did not offer collectors so ready an opportunity of competition, and probably also because their authenticity was even more difficult to determine, but they were prized and found their place in the volumes in which the prints were pasted. They were mentioned in the growing literature which was published for the instruction of the collectors of prints and, more important, they were reproduced in facsimile. They were probably the first English drawings to receive this honour, which had hitherto been reserved for the old masters. In the earliest book for the collector, the result of much collaboration, which appeared in 1781 as the *Biographical Anecdotes of Hogarth* over the name of J. Nichols, and went into three editions in four years, the writer, speaking of a drawing by Hogarth for a play-bill, which was still preserved, wishes that it were engraved, since his slightest sketch would be welcome to the numerous collectors of his works.

In the *Anecdotes of Hogarth*, of 1833, in which the investigations of the preceding two generations were summarized, a separate section is devoted to the drawings. By that date, the leading collector of Hogarth's works was H. P. Standly, of Paxton Place, St. Neots, who had several of his drawings engraved in facsimile for his own purposes. His collection was considerably enriched after the date of this book, chiefly from the Esdaile and Horace Walpole sales in 1840 and 1842. When it was sold in 1845, many of the drawings were bought for the Royal Library, which had several already in the magnificent collection of prints formed for George IV at Carlton House. Others passed, eventually, to the British Museum, where they joined gradually acquired accumulations. Meanwhile, the third important collection mentioned in the *Anecdotes* of 1833, that formed before 1793 and largely direct from Hogarth's widow by the ninth Earl of Exeter, remained and still remains at Burghley House, but except for the drawings reproduced in facsimile by Richard Livesay in 1781 and 1782, it seems not to have been known. With its publication in full, by the great kindness of the Marquis and Marchioness of Exeter, joined to that of the drawings in the Royal Library and the British Museum and some which have crossed the Atlantic, it is possible to reconstruct the greater part of the series known to have existed at the end of the eighteenth century, and to form a canon of Hogarth's draughtsmanship by which other drawings as they appear may be tested.

By no means all the drawings which were mentioned in the *Anecdotes* or have otherwise a good tradition behind them can be accepted as genuine; many, indeed, are obviously false. Hogarthian scholarship was largely literary, and the authority of a plausible story would have been accepted in preference to the evidence of the eyes, even if the work of his contemporaries had been better known. Until recognized in the *Anecdotes* as clearly engravers' drawings, the two copies of *Marriage a la Mode*, scenes III and IV, at Windsor, were held to be star-pieces in the best collections. One drawing from the Dyce collection at the Victoria and Albert Museum now rests more securely under the Dutch name of Aertsen, while, at the British Museum, besides drawings with most respectable histories which have long since been transferred to Mercier and Highmore, another, mentioned in the *Anecdotes* as then in the Sheepshanks collection, disclosed itself, when examined for the purpose of the present publication under the brilliant fluorescent light of its war-time home, to be in the main Italian of the sixteenth century; and all doubt was removed by the discovery of Italian words on the back when it was taken

Fig. 1. Sir James Thornhill: The Thornhill Family with Hogarth and others. Pen and violet wash.
The Marquess of Exeter

from its mount on its return to London. Except where a drawing is clearly connected with a print or picture, tradition must be the chief guide to authenticity. If, then, tradition proves untrustworthy, as in the cases quoted, the drawings which are labelled Hogarth in public and private collections without even the shadow of its authority, must be regarded with the utmost caution.[1]

The first and most striking feature of the collection is that it is very small. The painter who prided himself on displaying mankind in his natural form, and who heaped into his canvases such accumulations of character, costume and accessory, might well be expected to have habitually made sketches of men and manners as he met with them, and then to have experimented, on paper, with variations of composition in order to present his incidents with as much force as possible. The first expectation has sometimes become glib assertion in recent writings by persons who have not looked into the facts. Even the author of the *Biographical Anecdotes*, writing in 1781, before Hogarth's own memoranda were made public, noted that 'he had heard that Hogarth continually took sketches from Nature; and it is natural to suppose that he did so'. A few instances could be given, notably sketches at Calais[2] or of an engraver in a salivation, the semi-caricatures of *Gabriel Hunt* (No. 30), *Ben Read* (No. 88) and *Wilkes* (No. 95), or the scenes in the *Tour* of 1732 (No. 29). But, for further evidence, the author quoted relied (p. 13) on the word of 'a gentleman still living who once observed him to draw something with his pencil on his finger-nail. Enquiring what had been his employment, he was shewn the countenance (a whimsical one) of a person who was then sitting in sight'. Subsequent commentators multiplied

---

[1] For deliberate imitations or forgeries, see J. T. Smith, *Nollekens and his Times*, ii, p. 348. A drawing by Laroon was exhibited as Hogarth's even in the 1934 Exhibition of British Art. Sandby, Hayman and Boitard are also confused with him, *cf Vasari Society*, vi, 35 on a *Conversation* at Truro which seems to owe its attribution to Hogarth largely to an absurd affiliation to the *Midnight Modern Conversation*.

[2] Hogarth himself speaks in his note on the print *Roast Beef of Old England* of 'memorandums' shown to the Authorities when he was arrested. (Add. MS. 27991, fol. 51.) Among Lord Exeter's prints is a red-chalk tracing of a 'Sketch of a French Captain riding Post. Dunkirk, 1744'.

this single instance into a constant habit, and could point for confirmation to a large collection of small heads which were supposed to have been transferred from the finger-nail to paper, and thence to have found a place in Hogarth's prints. Such of these heads as are now available—and they have the authority of a most discriminating collector in other fields than Hogarth, William Esdaile—prove to be, at any rate in much the greater part, copies from the prints themselves.[3] This does not, however, disprove the story. Hogarth may have used for quick notation the convenient surface, as every schoolboy knows, for depicting human features in a naturally formed frame; but the mere fact that he had recourse to this device as well as the story that he called for pen and paper when he wished to draw Ben Read at the Bedford Arms Tavern, confirms the evidence of the extant drawings that Hogarth did not carry with him the sketch-book or tablets with which more normally constituted painters generally provided themselves.

There is a still greater lack of drawings which can be regarded as studies, whether from life or memory, for figures in prints or pictures of contemporary manners. It is only by an act of scholiast's association, as far-fetched as the identification of characters in the 'Button's Coffee House' drawings (Nos. 14–17) that the figures at Windsor (No. 18) have been called first thoughts for the *Harlot's Progress* and the *Happy Marriage*. There is a group of drawings which were certainly used in pictures or prints of scriptural or classical subjects. Of these, the St. Paul in red chalk at Burghley (No. 68) does not seem to be a life-study, but a trial in the manner of the old masters before proceeding to the picture at Lincoln's Inn. On the other hand, the nude woman (No. 25) and the *Hymen* (No. 26) appear to be academic exercises made in the life-school and afterwards adapted for the picture or print rather than drawings from models specially posed for the purpose of the compositions, and the *Man Levering a Rock* (No. 84) which was used for a figure in the Bristol Altarpiece may have had a similar origin. There is, however, only one drawing which has the air of a deliberate study from life, or rather, from memory, for a character in some contemporary scene. That is the *Fat Man upset like a Turtle* in Lord Exeter's collection (No. 78), and in this case no use is made of the figure in any known work.

Preparatory sketches, or rather drafts, of compositions form the larger proportion of the drawings, small as the total is. Here a new feature of interest is introduced. Only two out of the whole number, the *Beggars' Opera* (No. 23) and the *Falstaff* (No. 24) both described as from 'Hogarth's Sketch-book' are for subject pictures, and it is not merely accidental that they were stage-scenes, not the artist's compositions. There is not a single study on paper for such crowded scenes as the *Southwark Fair* and the *March to Finchley*, nor even for the most sustained of all Hogarth's productions, the *Marriage a la Mode* or the *Election* series.[4] Indeed, it may be said that, with the exception of the two stage-

---

[3] British Museum 1887–10–10–9 and 10, fifteen heads from Esdaile's Collection rightly catalogued as copies. They were, presumably, in the Bale Collection (Sale, Christie's 16 May 1881, Lot 405, 'fifteen heads from Esdaile's Collection', bought by Hogarth £4 10s.). Those which are identifiable are all in the same direction as the prints, as are the five from the Spielmann Collection (Christie's, 31 July 1947, Lot 185), also from Esdaile. See also on No. 89.

[4] The similarity between the lightly painted skull in the third scene of the *Marriage a la Mode* and the very elaborate pencil drawing at the Tate Gallery (Cat. No. 2220) can only be a coincidence. The brush drawing of Plate 8 of the *Rake's Progress* at the Victoria and Albert Museum (D.G. 5f 625) though not, as catalogued, a copy from the engraving, as is shown by the direction, is the engraver's drawing from the picture. It is closely incised and no doubt by one of the assistants employed for this series. It may be the 'beautiful and most valuable drawing in indian ink' of this scene, stated in *Anecd.* 1833, p. 394, to have then been in the possession of John Knowles, and may subsequently have been in the Standly Collection (Sale 1845, Lot 1211, bought by Tiffin for £3 13s. 6d.). Were it Lot 801 in the R. Udny Sale (Philipe, 1803), 'the original drawing for one of the plates of the *Rake's Progress*, pen and indian ink, highly finished', it would probably bear Udny's mark. The washed drawing connected with 'the Debauch plate' which was in the Willett Collection and the engraving from it by White (*Anecd.* 1833, p. 315) are both untraceable, as is the red chalk drawing of a figure for the *Rake's Progress*, 'with another study of the same on the reverse side', which formed Lot 103 in the Capel-Cure Sale (bought by Tregaskis £2 10). It was previously No. 1289 in the Esdaile Sale, bought Fuller 5s. The story told by J. T. Smith, *Nollekens and his Times*, ii, p. 346, regarding the 'Debauch plate' that Hogarth drew the wine-squirting incident in his sketch-book on the spot for the delectation of his companion Hayman, amounts to a *reductio ad absurdum* of the legends about his drawing from the life.

scenes, there are neither sketches nor studies of composition on paper where there are, or were, paintings in oil. On the other hand, there is a whole series of studies for the *Industry and Idleness* prints, and preparations of greater or lesser completeness for the *Hudibras* illustrations, the *Cruelty* series, and for several single prints or pairs, for all of which there were no pictures. The obvious inference is that Hogarth, who was nothing if not business-like, worked out the subjects of his prints on paper only when there would be no market for them as paintings in oil. Even when his sequences of prints had proved most successful, he had not secured, for all his novelties of salesmanship, satisfactory prices for the oil-paintings from which they had been made. In his most sanguine moments he could scarcely expect anybody to wish to place on his walls as many as a dozen oil paintings depicting the contrasted fortunes of two city-apprentices, nor the four agglomerations of horrors in which he built up his cautionary account of the *Progress of Cruelty* from the torture of animals to the dissecting table. Apparently, when he had paintings in view, he sometimes made preparatory studies in oil which he discarded. After them, and probably more often without them, he outlined his compositions on the canvas, as the picture on an easel in his early self-portrait and extant examples show. Often he must have changed his mind or added further telling details as the picture progressed, just as he did on paper with his drawings, or even on the copper of his prints. But the two drawings for oil paintings, which are exceptions to his general rule, show how close his first thoughts came to the final composition. Once he had formulated his composition in his mind, he proceeded directly to his canvas without preparatory study on paper of either single figures or the whole composition. This may seem almost miraculous, but Hogarth had faith in himself to perform miracles, and his paintings only too often have the air of improvisation.

The rarity of Hogarth's drawings cannot be explained by supposing that the bulk have been lost or destroyed, nor would this account for the disproportion between the number for engravings and that for pictures. The well-known story that he threw the sketch of Wilkes into the fire (see on No. 95) appears to be due to a confusion with another incident, when he is said to have thrown either the memory drawing of Fielding or the facsimile etching by Basire into the fire, mistaking one for the other. In either case, his wife's cousin was at hand to rush in and save it from the flames. He certainly made presents of his drawings, but the friends who forced them from him, to use Walpole's phrase, are not likely to have treated them as valueless. Some were given back to his widow, who gave them away again or sold them. After her death, her sale in 1790 contained very few drawings, and one 'parcel of academy figures and studies by Mr. Hogarth and others'. The early commentators, besides enumerating the drawings known to them, made careful lists of Hogarth's friends and other collectors from whom they had obtained information, and it is unlikely that they or others owned many more drawings than were then specified. Horace Walpole believed when Hogarth gave him his drawings for *Industry and Idleness* and an oil sketch of the Committee that these were the artist's last remaining sketches. He was mistaken, but his belief shows that either Hogarth did not make studies of figures or incidents, or that, if he did, he did not retain them, as other artists do, for future use, but valued them less, and kept them less long, than his more finished preparations.

But it is idle to speculate about the possible loss or destruction of Hogarth's drawings. He himself has explained why they are so few. In his manuscript drafts for an autobiography which are now in the British Museum he tells us that he drew so little from nature, and maintained that it was so little necessary to do so, that a brother artist turned his doctrine to ridicule by saying: 'The only way to learn to draw well is never to draw at all'.[5] Another fragment suggests that he himself expressed his views in these words—perhaps to annoy old Richardson, to whom drawings were 'the very spirit and quint-

---

[5] Egerton MS. 3015, fol. 9.

essence of the art', or Allan Ramsay, who made exquisite studies of heads and hands in chalk on paper before placing them on canvas—and that his words led, as he writes, 'some wagish [*sic*] friend' to reply: 'Yes, and the best way to learn to swim is not to go to the water'. In sentences which have been neglected by his modern biographers as much as have the drawings themselves, Hogarth tells us that learning to draw in the ordinary way would have taken him too long, and that it would have interfered too much with his pleasures if he had occupied himself with sketching when he was abroad. No doubt as he was tied, when a young man, all day to his silver-chasing and routine engraving, he needed relaxation after hours, but he was also too keenly interested in human nature to interpose a sketch-book between himself and life. Besides, the power to represent what he saw with more or less accuracy came to him so easily, and with so little conscious learning, that he regarded drawing from nature as scarcely distinguishable from copying the work of other men.

'In order, therefore, that his pleasures and his studies might go hand in hand' he set about to store his mind with images and, since 'drawing and painting are only a much more complicated form of writing' he endeavoured to construct from that store an alphabet of forms which could be combined and manipulated as easily and with as much meaning as the letters from which words are composed. Further, and no doubt with some memory of his father, who had written and published an examination of the eight parts of speech in English and Latin with the title *Disputationes Grammaticales*, he had the ambition of going beyond an alphabet and constructing a grammar of forms. It only remained to find subjects on which to devote the fullness of his mind.

In another draft,[6] which seems to have been composed for the instruction of an amateur in landscape, perhaps for someone whom he had offered to teach, as he did Mrs. Delany in 1732,[7] 'by some rule of his own that he says will improve me more in a day than a year's teaching in the ordinary way', he gives a warning that the hand must be methodically practised in putting down what the mind has stored. Otherwise the impressions would be effaced and the sketcher would be in the same plight as a person who might 'know the words and their meaning and yet never be able to write, lacking the hand to perform'. This would appear from other drafts[8] to have been his own early practice, but in a more definitive statement of his 'doctrine' in a draft annexed as a preface to the third manuscript of the *Analysis*,[9] and followed shortly after by the *reductio ad absurdum* mentioned above, he writes as though his method demanded no preliminary work in pencil. It was to 'collect and retain a remembrance of what I saw by repeated observation, only trying now and then upon my canvas how far I was advanced by that means'. If, as he says in still another draft under an erasure, he (sometimes) 'took the life for correcting the parts that I had not perfectly enough remembered when I came to put them in practice', he confesses that he did so 'too seldom'.[10]

Hogarth is explicit that the technical memory thus developed was linear in character. He is known to have delighted in such epitomes as the three lines with which one of the Carracci is said to have indicated a disappearing soldier with his pike and his dog, and he is reported to have once stopped in admiration

---

[6] Add. MSS. 27991, f. 11 verso and f. 13.   [7] *Autobiography*, 1861, vol. I, p. 283.

[8] Add. MSS. 27993, fol. 14.   [9] Egerton, 3015, f. 9.

[10] Add. MSS. 27991, fol. 12. J. Ireland (*Hogarth Illustrated*, III, 12) uses the phrase 'coldly copying on the spot' whereas the MSS. reads 'without drawing' or 'without directly drawing' and 'on the spot' or 'at the time', and he substitutes 'and then I transferred them to my composition' for 'when I came to put them in practice'. It was inevitable that he should alter and embroider in contriving his clever patchwork. A striking instance is his importation (*ibid.*, p. 350) of a reference to Paris into Hogarth's account of his print *Roast Beef of Old England*. Here, as on the words 'coldly copying' he goes further and appends a note. This gloss, though emphatically corrected in *Anecd.* 1833 (p. 317) and questioned by Austin Dobson (1907, p. 100) has misled the catalogue of the National Gallery (1946) in the note on the picture (No. 1464, p. 71).
For a full account of Hogarth's manuscripts we must await the publication of Mr. Joseph Burke's careful examination. I hope that I have not unduly trespassed upon his domain.

Fig. 2.   Figures from pl. 2 of the Analysis of Beauty: FIRST SCORE OF LINES FOR THE WEDDING DANCE (71); A COUNTRY DANCE (123); THE MINUET (122)

before a St. George and the Dragon scrawled in straight lines on a wall. To show how few lines are necessary to give the general idea of figures and actions, he describes in chapter xvi, p. 136, of the *Analysis* the manner in which he began to set out the design of the country dance which forms the chief feature of his second plate. Possibly he may have used some such symbols, mentally or on paper, to assist his memory, but he writes as though he began this, his 'first score of lines' by setting out letters and simple forms (fig. 2), and then chose figures and actions to fit them. Even allowing that he only wished to present pairs of figures in contrast, without any suggestion of a general action, it would seem that such symbols could mean nothing unless a strong visual memory and highly characterized figures were behind them. Nor is there any idea of a scheme of composition underlying their juxta-position. Something of the kind might, indeed, have served for the interwoven patterning of form which is seen in the admirable drawing of *The Operation* (No. 65), and would be a marked feature of certain groups in the *March to Finchley* and *Chairing the Member* if they had not been swamped by the unruly mobs thrown round them, but there is nothing of this here. When Hogarth comes some pages later to the 'hay' figure in the country dance in which (p. 150) the couples interweave and thus form a number of serpentine lines interlacing, and which, if it had been displayed as perhaps was originally intended,[11] in his second plate, would have embodied everything that the *Analysis* set out to show, he has to resort to another scheme altogether, and it and the scheme of a minuet above it are more like choreographer's diagrams than hints to a designer or a help to visual memory. In telling us that he made up his pictures by adding figure to figure in order to contrast their characters, Hogarth confesses to the chief weakness of his compositions.

A passage in the Introduction to the *Analysis* was intended to make clear Hogarth's conception of form as a combination of lines and thereby, incidentally, to assist the reader in cultivating a technical memory, but it has only led to more obscurity. He there suggests that the lines which compose forms may best be grasped by imagining oneself to see them from within, as though one were standing inside them, or, by an analogy which he uses in his table of contents to epitomize the whole chapter, 'by considering solid objects as only thin shells composed of lines like the outer coat of an onion'. In elaborating this 'conceit, as it may be called by some', Hogarth has been taken by a recent writer, Mr. Joseph Burke,[12] to be explicitly basing his aesthetic on the modern doctrine of 'Empathy' which is defined for this purpose, somewhat inadequately, as the mental process 'by which the spectator identifies himself with the object he looks at, is uplifted by the mountain and soothed by the calm lake'. Nothing could be further from Hogarth's thought. The whole of this illustration, as of the treatise generally, is strictly visual and external in its nature. Hogarth carefully explains that the combination of lines which makes up the inside of the shell coincides exactly with that of the outside. The main purpose of the passage is to introduce at the outset his view of objects as made up of lines. He was aware (p. 94) that there are no

---

[11] As it appears to be in the well-known oil prototype of the print, which is in the Camberwell Art Gallery.

[12] *Hogarth and Reynolds*, Oxford, 1943.

lines in nature and, therefore, was forced to recognize that mezzotint prints, if they could 'be wrought as accurately as those with the graver', would, for this reason, have the advantage over line engravings. But himself an engraver first and foremost, he was entirely occupied with lines and the whole of his great discovery that the principle of beauty resided in the character of lines arose out of his profession and practice. The title of his treatise was originally 'The Analysis of Beauty *or Forms lineally considered*', and it is, perhaps, unfortunate that the words in italics were omitted when the book was sent to press. Knowing that his ideas would appear too abstract and unfamiliar, he added the Introduction, which is not in the first three drafts, to his Treatise; and in this particular passage his recommendation that one should, in imagination, place oneself inside an object in order to grasp its component lines is nothing more than an effort to explain to the completely uninstructed that the whole of an object, with its back and its front, is never seen from the outside. One contour disappears as another appears; it is only from the inside that a sphere is visible as a complete circle in three dimensions, or, as he puts it, 'as circumscribed or wound about' at the extremities of equal lines from the centre 'with close connected threads, or lines, forming a true spherical shell'.

In so far as the doctrine of 'Empathy' has a general validity, Hogarth, like every other painter, must manifest its phenomena in his work. Indeed, in its most rudimentary form—that of the artist or the spectator mentally throwing himself into the physical attitude or action of the person represented—he may have been more influenced by it than others, since he relied so greatly upon his memory rather than on the model or on sketches. He may well have assumed, consciously or unconsciously, with or without the mirror, the expressions on the faces and the attitudes of the personages whom he was painting, though, considering the nature of his subjects, it is to be hoped that he did this but rarely. But in this passage of the *Analysis* he is not even hinting at this possibility. Mr. Burke, developing his idea and contrasting for the purposes of his essay the bases of Hogarth's and Reynolds's theories, speaks of the shock which must have been given to contemporary connoisseurs by Hogarth's invocation of so commonplace an object as an onion in this august context. Hogarth himself would have been much more shocked if another 'wagish' friend had told him that, according to his theory, he must identify himself with an onion in order to present it properly on his canvas.

Other references to drawing in Hogarth's writings are less baffling. In the chapter (x) of the *Analysis* where he develops his idea of the serpentine line as the principle of beauty in the human form, he speaks of legs which are so swollen with disease that all their serpentine lines are effaced as 'having lost their *drawing*, as the painters call it'. The italics are his. In two other notes, the rich confusion of ideas is characteristically Hogarthian. He is contrasting the 'inaccuracy' of his popular sets of prints, the *Industry and Idleness* and *Stages of Cruelty* with the 'fine strokes and soft engraving which require more care and practice than can often be obtained, except by a man of a very quiet turn of mind'. He excuses the imperfection partly on the ground of expense, which would have been too great for the purpose in view, but he also justifies it as 'hardness of execution addressed to hard hearts' 'the strong bold stroke' which expresses the passions, and 'the rude and hasty touch, when the fancy is warm' which 'gives a spirit not to be equalled by high finishing'. Hardness is applicable enough to the prints, but the other qualities are merely those which were generally accepted as virtues in a sketch. Certainly neither of the two series exhibits the rude and hasty touch, except, possibly, in the two subjects where the woodcuts produce some effect of spontaneity and speed by their savage contrasts of black and white, and these were executed by another hand and they were abandoned precisely because of their expense.

Strangely enough, one of the very subjects in the *Cruelty* series for which forcible execution would be most suitable, presents one of the best examples of 'fine drawing' in Hogarth's work. In the pencil drawing at Burghley for the *First Stage* (No. 70), everything, except the animals whose struggles have resulted in chaos, is set down gently, almost tenderly, and there is nothing either in the design or in the execution to suggest any emotion in the artist, or to communicate any feeling from him to the observer. In the elaborated version (No. 71) of this subject, in which, as in the *Beer Street* and *Gin Lane* (Nos. 76 and 77), everything tentative has been eliminated, the hardening of the outlines gives no more vigour to the touch, and the figures have become even more wooden and inexpressive apart from the activities in which they are observed to be engaged. The *Boys peeping* (No. 22) is another example of 'fine drawing', but here it is part of the convention of which the engraving is a parody. The most ambitious attempt at delicate pencil-work is to be found in the two heads from the antique and Fiammingo (Nos. 81 (*i*) and (*j*)) with which Hogarth sought, in the *Analysis*, to illustrate the predominance of fine serpentine lines in the most masterly renderings of the human face. Here, though the character of the heads, alien as they are to Hogarth's usual models, is admirably brought out, chiefly by the strong lines and contours, the modelling which is the chief purpose of the illustration shows by its uncertainty of touch and confusion of direction that Hogarth had not the patience nor the knowledge to effect with the pencil the subtleties which he could express so successfully with brush and pigment. Aware of his failure, he did not transfer his drawings to the copper, but confining himself to small and confessedly quite inadequate prints, he attempted to justify himself by declaring that it was beyond the powers of any engraving, however large, to express all that he had in mind.

Drawing or painting had a long way to travel from being 'merely a complicated manner of writing', in order to become a means of representing all the network of serpentine lines which constitute grace in the fairest works of nature or the great masters. Hogarth had no pride in showing himself to be consistent. He once surprised his friend the engraver Grignion with the outburst 'I never was right save when I had been wrong'. He was alternately the faithful portrayer of people as they were, the satirist of contemporary life and the would-be designer of tapestries or stained glass, the painter of sacred subjects on a heroic scale, and the writer who would set the world right with regard to the principles of beauty. To understand him at all, it is necessary to recognize his origins, first in his early training as silver-chaser and engraver, and then under the immediate influence of Thornhill. For the latter, there is his own statement that he was fired with the wish to paint by Thornhill's work at St. Paul's and Greenwich, and the debt is proclaimed by his use of Thornhill's formula for indicating the features of the face both in the chalk drawing of *Hymen* (No. 26) and in the head outlined on the canvas which replaced a crouching faun in the later, bowdlerized version of *Boys Peeping at Nature* (No. 22). The manner of Thornhill is apparent in the early illustrations to King's *Pantheon* (No. 1), in the satirical allegory of the *Lottery* (No. 2) and, strengthened by French influences, in the *Beggars' Opera Burlesqued* (No. 12), and the frontispiece to *Hudibras* (No. 5). The effects of the early practice of silver-chasing are even more evident in Hogarth's idea of ornamental line. The illustrations to King's *Pantheon* in their arrangement and with their borders might be designs for silver plaques or medallions and, whenever Hogarth breaks out into ornament, the waving and serpentine lines of his *Analysis* become mere shadows and weak echoes of his floridity. Flamboyance was part of his nature—it was possibly a symptom of the self-assertiveness which belonged to the 'five-foot man', as Vertue described him—and it was encouraged by the demand for extravagant ornament in contemporary silver and, at a slightly later stage, in trade-bills and shop designs. The design for a shop-bill at the British Museum (No. 85) may serve as an example, but it is only a preliminary sketch. For the mature development of his manner, it is necessary to turn to the chair which Hogarth designed for Garrick as president of the Shakespeare Club (fig. 3). It was conceived in all seriousness, and is said to have actually been executed, in honour of his friend, the actor, and of their common idol, the nation's pride. Samuel Ireland in illustrating it (*Graphic Illustrations* ii, 147) in a period of more restrained taste, describes it as somewhat surcharged with ornaments and too ponderous to exhibit much elegance of execution. In fact, even Kent, whom Hogarth loved to ridicule, can never have conceived anything equalling its monstrous accumulations. Yet this is only an extension, such as was due to its more honoured, almost ritual, purpose, of the ornamentation bestowed on the lawyer's stall in *Hudibras* (No. 8) or the throne in the print of *Henry VIII and Anne Boleyn*. Speaking generally, plain furniture with him is reserved for middle- and lower-class houses, it does not form part of the sumptuous mansions which he preferred to represent. No doubt, excessive floridity is as much a mark of the period as of Hogarth's individual mentality, but to understand fully one aspect of his art, even of his drawings, it is as necessary to keep this chair in mind as, for another aspect, to attempt—impossible though it be for the present day—to remember that he, in common with his whole generation, could read the poem of *Hudibras* from beginning to end with appreciation and even enjoyment. The combination of the two aspects, as in this design, without satire or humour but in serious admiration, results in a kind of grim grotesque, some form of which apparently appeals to each generation—only to disgust the next.

Hogarth's 'low shrubb instructions', to use Vertue's phrase,[13] as silver-chaser and cheap engraver, had lasting effects of a more far-reaching nature. For the ornamentation of silverware or trade cards, human forms were almost as much a heraldic stock-in-trade as the lions, stags or unicorns which figured with them on coats-of-arms or as supporters. Their main lines constituted as recognizable a notation, if they could be varied to

Fig. 3. THE SHAKESPEARE CHAIR.
Aquatint by Jane Ireland after Hogarth

a greater extent by attitude, attribute or accessory to express a wider series of allegorical or emblematic ideas. Nor was their use in the decoration of wallspaces very different. Hogarth naturally accepted the notation and, much as he may have laughed at the absurdities committed in the name of decoration or allegory, he can have had little notion of the long process of selection that the forms had undergone before they reached the shape which was accepted as the ideal, nor could he have appreciated the lengthy discipline and constant labour by means of which the painters of Italy or the Low Countries had striven to give real flesh and blood to the forms within the conventions. He came at a comparatively late stage to the meetings at St. Martin's Lane, and then, according to his own account, attended but half-heartedly and, instead of mastering the coherence of parts and the interaction of movements in the human body, the 'science' of drawing, as it was called, he accepted the forms as a kind of language and attempted to find a grammar to it. When he condemns copying from nature as from other painters because it teaches only to set down the part at which one is looking, he is not referring to the relation of each part to an organic whole, but to the copyist's failure to grasp the meaning, the intention of the model in that pose or action. The drawing for the early print of the *Lottery* shows him employing this language for satiric purposes as anonymous Dutchmen had lately done for the same

[13] *Walpole Society*, iii, 123.

events. From this to the use of minute contemporary figures as in the *South Sea Bubble* (No. 3) is but a gentle step, for which the same artists or Callot could supply precedents in plenty.

Even in his developed work, Hogarth displays his origin in this school, and is the product of precisely the group of ideas with which his example was afterwards contrasted. The criticism of the day condemned mere copying of nature because it was not aimed at the 'ideal', just as he did because it did not reveal a 'meaning'. Though he was well aware of the propensity of his public to discover ridicule of some famous or notorious character in every one of his figures, and though he owed some part of the popularity even of the *Harlot's Progress* to a supposed portrait of a well-known prostitute-hunter in the third plate, Hogarth maintained that he represented no real persons in his social scenes. Individual as they may have seemed to contemporaries, his personages are always intended to stand for the characteristics which he wishes to ridicule or to use for the illustration of some moral. When he contrasts, in the *Analysis*, a waterman with Charon, he explains that one is as much the personification of a particular kind of strength as the other; if he paints a handsome young woman or an elegant young man, they embody for him the qualities of Beauty and Grace as does a classical Venus or Antinous. He makes their meaning clearer by heaping up accessory and attribute, just as did the painters of the ideal, and can even help himself, as they could but rarely, by means of written words. His introduction into one scene of different stages of a story instead of concentrating upon the dramatic incident all the resources of lighting and composition may seem the return to a more primitive form of art; in reality, it is the product of the discursive decorative conventions in which he was brought up. He was completely at one with his contemporaries in regarding 'Expression' as the summit of a painter's ambition, the ultimate test of his skill. His large scriptural compositions, with their partial and occasional intrusion of 'nature', are not an excrescence on his work, commissions alien to his genius and forced on him for gain, they are only manifestations in another sphere of his aims in his contemporary representations.

When he uses the pen on a large scale in his preliminary sketches, Hogarth retains much of the floridity of his ornamental manner. It betrays itself in the loose open curves in which his hand moves, though the lines are scratchy at times or tremulous, and always broken, either because unsure of their direction or to appear artless by their avoidance of calligraphic fluency. His line is descriptive, rather than searching or incisive, but descriptive of action or movement rather than of form and, therefore, merely approximate and careless of structure. A scramble of cross lines serves to suggest bulk when it is not effected by means of wash. Even when, as nearly always, the pen follows pencil work or rough tracing, it seems consciously hurried or careless, as though he wished at once to exhibit the liveliness of his fancy and to impart vitality to his figures and the scene. He may have wished to display in his own words the 'rude and hasty touch of the warm fancy', but his manner remains the same whether the passions are present or absent; whether the artist is moved or indifferent, his chief aim is the appearance of extemporary spontaneity.

Where, as in the drawings of the *Tour* of 1732 (No. 29), merely light-hearted records of forms and action are intended, the floridity is to some extent suppressed and the sketches are merely rough and undistinguished, without mastery either of movement or contour; they need the much greater sophistication of Rowlandson's line to give them point. When fantasy entered, in the tail-piece, and he had the opportunity to caricature a mask and ornament such as might have been found on the handle of a basin or ewer, the result is full rhetoric. The drawing of an opera singer, wrongly called *Farinelli* (No. 4), may not be his, but in any case the parody in the manner entered with the subject, and there is not a trace of the wit, either in form or expression, which marks the Italian caricatures of similar subjects. In the *Hudibras* drawings, where he is dealing for the most part with exaggerated forms in vehement action, he proceeds by means of bulges and empty curves which weaken instead of strengthening his figures. It is possible that, if his drawings were more numerous, Hogarth might be seen in them to be developing, with growing mastery, from floridity towards simplicity. At any rate, the pen drawings in the *Analysis* are direct enough, and in one of the most fully autographic of all his drawings, the *Garrick and Quin compared* of 1746 (No. 39), the curves are restrained and the drawing cleaner. But neither it nor the drawings of the *Analysis* are meant in any way to be expressive, they are diagrammatic rather than descriptive. Further, one of his latest drawings, which is in chalk and not in pen, the *New Order of Architecture* (No. 94), is perhaps the most pompous and inflated in all his work.

Hogarth's handling of the pen is best exemplified in the one large series of drawings, that for the *Industry and Idleness* of 1747, since in some of them successive stages can be followed, and in all the final product is also there for comparison. It is, perhaps, just because he was little moved either by ridicule or indignation that he there took more pains than usual in choice of subject and in developing his compositions. In the seventh scene (Nos. 51–53) where, almost alone in Hogarth's work, some sympathy seems to be shown with poverty and extreme distress of mind, the misery finds expression in a flattened line and the dragging of the pen, but elsewhere, though the forms necessarily differ according as, for example, the idle apprentice is gambling on a tombstone or his antitype singing hymns, yet the artist's hand is not moved either by horror or admiration; it shows nothing but haste to set out his idea, without thought of 'meaning' or accuracy of contour. These features are studiously emphasized in the final preparations for the prints, but at such sacrifice of vigour in comparison with the earlier drafts that in one case, at least, the *Execution Scene* (No. 63), some doubt may justifiably be felt regarding Hogarth's complete authorship. Where there are the successive drafts of the subjects, it is possible to follow the workings of Hogarth's mind as well as of his hand. In some, for example the scene already quoted, he started with little more than a group of two figures in a dismal bedroom examining ill-gotten spoil. Already at this stage he probably had the notion, corresponding to the text from the Bible ultimately printed on the plate, of the guilty startled by a noise, but the idea had not yet found the pictorial shape which it gained in the subsequent drafts. In the tenth plate (Nos. 60–62) he gradually enriches both the dramatic and the scenic effects of the incident but, whether he began with or without any idea of the physical relations of his personages to each other, he ends without any spatial realization of the scene. In other drawings, the *Banquet Scene* (No. 54) and the *Betrayal* (Nos. 58 and 59), he begins with the memory of some actual scene or picture, and it is not until a later stage that the principal character or the dramatic incidents enter at all. In the *Marriage Scene* (Nos. 49 and 50) the development is largely pictorial, and consists in the rearrangement of subsidiary characters, while the three discarded subjects (Nos. 55–57), although among the best of the drawings, were regarded as either too cryptic or too banal to be developed at all. The two versions of the *Operation in a Hospital* (Nos. 64 and 65) conjecturally connected with this series, stand alone for the sensitive delineation and the elegance of the pencil-work and light wash, and, if it were not that the subject is characteristically Hogarthian and that he must be allowed a greater liberty in manner than is usual with draughtsmen, there would be a suspicion that the more emptily decorative elaboration betrayed a different hand. But in all the other preliminary drawings, the same characteristics appear, a forcible, somewhat ungainly summarization of general form and action with an exuberance which is partly the relic of a tradition and partly the *bravura* of real or assumed spontaneity.

Possibly, Hogarth found the pen irksome with its likeness to the graving tool and its constant reminder of the delicacy with which it could be profitably employed by a quieter mind than his. He found its incisiveness valuable for his rare personal caricatures such as the *Ben Read* (No. 88) or the *Wilkes* (No. 95), and for that purpose, perhaps, used an old and rusty implement as he did when contrasting character with caricature (No. 108). But he despised caricature, holding it good precisely in proportion to the absence from it of recognizable representation. On the whole, the pen was for him as for most artists of the period mainly useful in giving precision and permanence to lines already drawn

Fig. 3a (Cat. No. 116).   After Hogarth: The Bruiser and
Giants in Guildhall. Etching by J. Mills

with the pencil. For his first thoughts and more or less careless formulation of his visual ideas, chalk was a better medium, possessing much of the freedom and something of the elasticity of the brush. Sometimes he used red chalk for the most careful of his cartoons for engravings, either with elaborate hatching and fine lines, as in the *Hudibras Sallying Forth* (No. 6), or with firm outline as in the *Cruelty* series, the *Beer Street* and *Gin Lane* (Nos. 71–73, 75–77), or with the woolly amplitude of the *New Order of Architecture* (No. 94). But for any of these, the pen and wash of the finished drawings for the *Industry and Idleness* would have served equally well. The truly characteristic use of chalk appears in the two large drawings 'from Hogarth's sketch-book' for his *Beggars' Opera* and *Falstaff* (Nos. 23 and 24). In them, if any-where, Hogarth is merely placing on the paper in juxtaposition forms which he probably retained in memory from the scene on the stage. It was, no doubt, with chalk that he first tried the power of his technical memory on the canvas, fixing the lines where they were satis-factory with the brush and a thin fluid pigment and giving, at that stage, a correctness of contour which was not required from the first chalk outline. In these drawings, he is not disturbed by any problems of accuracy such as weakened and, indeed, defeated him in the 'academies' of the same sketch-book, nor by any consideration either of 'beauty' or of moral purpose, nor even by the desire to express that 'character' which he was always so determined to depict to the last ounce; the forms and character and action are sufficiently indicated by his vigorous approximations. Were it not for certain obvious disproportions and uncertainties, the correction of which weakens the picture, the sketch for the *Beggars' Opera* would more than give promise of the mastery which Hogarth intermittently exhibited at different periods of his career in the *Conquest of Mexico*, the *Marriage à la Mode*, and the *Election* series.

On a smaller scale, the virtues of Hogarth's chalk drawing are even more signally exhibited in two sketches, one of which, unfortunately, is only known at present through a facsimile. Both the drawing for the *Jacobite's Journal* (No. 67) and that for a small inset in the *Bruiser* (No. 116) are of a very slight and casual nature and both were inspired, as was the drawing of Wilkes, by political animosity, even personal hatred. Here there is no voluntary nor involuntary flourish of the pen nor possibility of elabora-tion with the pencil. The heat of the idea has found immediate expression. If there is any consciousness of the medium or of the manner, it may be that Hogarth had in his mind in the latter drawing the reed pen or chalk sketches of Rembrandt, which were well known to the connoisseurs of the day, and admired for just the same reasons as they are now. Hogarth ridiculed him as a dark and dirty old master,

Fig. 4-7. HEADS FROM AN UNFINISHED PAINTING
(4) "MR. HOGARTH". (5) "LAVINIA FENTON". (6) A BOY. (7) "HANDEL".
Actual size. The Marquess of Exeter

but this was a satire of a despicable subject and for its expression Hogarth may well have thought fit to adopt methods which he considered unworthy of more serious employment.

Later in the century, when caricature was at its height, the virtues of rough, even of purposely 'bad' drawing came to be widely appreciated; and already, in his day, the spirited sketch was valued by the connoisseur as generally more effective than the finished product. Hogarth was aware of this, but he was not drawing for the cabinet of the connoisseur. His finished drawings are stages towards engravings which were intended for the common man. For that audience it was necessary to be articulate in every syllable. Walpole could write in disgust to Gray in 1753, of a higher public than that which Hogarth addressed, that 'they want as much to have the words "A Man, a Cock" written under his (Bentley's) drawings, as under the most execrable hieroglyphics of Egypt or sign-post painters'. A plain man who was not even familiar with a form in outline would make nothing of an arm or a leg which was indicated merely by a couple of nervous lines, he would demand five fingers on each hand, a neatly-turned calf and, above all, a face which possessed a nose and a mouth as well as a pair of recognizable eyes, and not merely, as in Rembrandt's drawings, a couple of dots so perfectly placed that they give the structure of the head as well as the direction and dramatic intensity of the glances. Even if he had had the patience and the power, Hogarth could not have felt sure that he could convey his meaning by the mere concentration of his action and the interrelation of his personages with the emphasis of design and the light and shade of their setting. Hence the rigid precision of the outline, the shadowy personages in the background who have no part as yet in the visual scene but indicate the consequences of the action, the heaped accessories which may have delighted the artist's consciousness in themselves, but certainly served primarily to help the observer to piece out the story, the explanatory writings which are less crude than the balloons issuing from the mouths of characters in the popular prints, but are always so placed that they are legible to the beholder and not to the personages in the picture. Hence, too, the insistence on facial expression which was the first quality for Hogarth as for his contemporaries and predecessors, and on which he based his triumphant claims. He supplied his public not only with the strip-picture and the caption, but also, and above all, with the close-up.

Hogarth's drawings are too few and too diverse to allow of easy and clear-cut generalizations about his character. But in their very diversity they reflect the contradictions which made up his strange personality, while their rarity is, in itself, illuminating. He was a 'natural' draughtsman as he was a painter, so much so, indeed, that, in common with others of his period, he tended to disregard an abnormal gift as something within the power of everyone. Hazlitt went too far in saying that 'he never looks at any object but to find out a moral or a ludicrous effect'.[14] The four exquisite little heads at Burghley, evidently cut from an unfinished canvas (Figs. 4-7), here reproduced for the first time, with their traditional titles, should serve as a welcome reminder of the sympathy with which he could, when he wished, portray his fellow creatures. But it is true that he seldom draws or paints a figure or movement either for its own sake or for the sake of the drawing itself. He looked upon drawing as merely a species of copying and, in maintaining that it was worthless and empty except in so far as it conveyed a meaning or a moral, he was merely substituting an everyday notion of a language for the current doctrine that Dutch accuracy and fidelity to nature were low and valueless because they did not possess the element of the ideal. To this end, the painters loaded their figures with conventional beauties and emblematic attributes while he accumulated telling accessories and forced action and expression. Nature, too, would have 'put him out'. For his moral subjects and to some extent for the ridiculous, nature could have offered no opportunity to 'copy' precisely those momentary[15] effects which he needed

---

[14] On Mr. Wilkie's pictures. *The Champion*, March 5, 1815 (*Works*, xi, 247), quoted by Austin Dobson (1907), p. 84.

[15] Hogarth refers to the value of his technical doctrine for noting momentary effects. (Add. MSS. 27991, fol. 1 verso.)

for his purpose. He was also too literal when in front of the object. In his portraits the sitters wear too often the strained expression or the vacant smile with which they faced the artist from the model's chair, and their attitudes are either dull and insipid or jerked into agitation by the painter in order to produce an effect of life. Similarly, though only based on memory, his actors in the subject pictures are frequently so intent upon exhibiting their character that they forget their places in the action. The reason that Hogarth's paintings are accused of theatricality may well lie in this propensity of his personages to look away from the action and across the footlights in order to exhibit their poses to the audience and so attract their applause. Consequently, he is seen at his best in his sketches where his abnormal power of memory summoned up some scene which had struck him as especially horrible or ridiculous. For this purpose the brush served him better than pencil, pen, or even chalk, because of the immediacy of its effect. It tempts less, also, to the elaborate detail to which Hogarth was forced by his desire to tell his story and point his moral by piling up expression and meaning. Nor, whether with the pencil or the brush, could his power of representing the figure often stand by itself. He had not the quiet mind, as he himself said, nor would he take the trouble, for the thorough study of form which is necessary for perfect draughtsmanship. Vigorous characterization and action with an obvious purpose can mask, especially in a sketch, imperfect command of form or even the positive bad drawing with which an eighteenth-century writer, more sensitive to form than ourselves, could tax Hogarth in his engravings. Moreover, the effort of accurate and complete characterization probably tired him, and he seldom maintains the same level of execution throughout a picture. Even so, he has created figures which satisfy the most critical eye as well as the appetite of the common reader of anecdotic subject pictures. In the end, much as the more sophisticated critic may strive to sustain Hogarth's high position by basing it on his *Shrimp Girl* or the few drawings and oil sketches that have come down to us, it is to his prints, with all their imperfections, and the subject series with their, in general, indifferent composition and forced drama, that he owes his claim to immortality. Time and unfamiliarity have removed the offence of his personages and softened the ridicule or the horror of his scenes, and have invested them with a proverbial, almost classically generalized, humanity which comes very near to the idealism which he derided and despised. Time, too, has given mellowness and beauty to the colour which his contemporaries universally condemned, and has thus requited him for all the abuse that he poured upon it, in a manner that he can never have expected at its hands.

BIBLIOGRAPHY

[John Nichols, George Steevens, Isaac Reed, etc.] :
Biographical Anecdotes of William Hogarth, 1781, 1782, and 1785. (Referred to as *Biogr. Anec.*, 1781, etc.)

John Ireland: *Hogarth Illustrated*, vols. 1 and 2, 1791, vol. 3, 1798. (*Hog. Illd.*)

Samuel Ireland: *Graphic Illustrations of Hogarth*, vol. 1, 1794, vol. 2, 1799. (*Graph. Illust.*)

John Nichols and George Steevens: *The Genuine Works of William Hogarth*, vols. 1 and 2, 1808-1810; vol. 3, 1817. (*Gen. Works.*)

[John Bowyer Nichols] : *Anecdotes of William Hogarth*, 1833. (*Anecd.*, 1833)

Austin Dobson and Sir William Armstrong: *William Hogarth*, 1902. (*A.D.*, 1902)

Austin Dobson: *William Hogarth*, 1907. (*A.D.*, 1907)

British Museum: *Catalogue of Political and Personal Satires*, vols. II-IV, 1873-1883. (*B.M. Sat.*)

British Museum: *Drawings by British Artists*, vol. II, 1900. (*L.B.*)

Pierpont Morgan Collection of Drawings by the Old Masters, vol. III, 1912.

PRINCIPAL SALE CATALOGUES

Mrs. Hogarth	... ...	Greenwood ...	... 24 April 1790 (reprinted *Burlington Magazine*, Oct. 1944).
S. Ireland ...	... ...	Christies' ...	... 6 May 1797.
S. Ireland ...	... ...	Sotheby's ...	... 7 May 1801.
J. Ireland ...	... ...	King & Lochee	... 5 March 1810.
George Baker	... ...	Sotheby's ...	... 16 June 1825.
W. Esdaile ...	... ...	Christies' ...	... 18 June 1840.
Horace Walpole	... ...	Robins ...	... 13 June 1842.
H. P. Standly	... ...	Christies' ...	... 14 April 1845.
Dr. Wellesley	... ...	Sotheby's ...	... 25 June 1866.
F. Capel-Cure	... ...	Sotheby's ...	... 15 May 1905.

THE CATALOGUE

CATALOGUE OF HOGARTH'S DRAWINGS

1. DESIGNS FOR KING'S *PANTHEON*   Fig. 8-10
                                    Royal Library (13468-70)

Drawings for three of the six plates, each containing four designs, in reverse, without name of artist or engraver, illustrating an edition of King's *Pantheon* (first published in 1710).

(*a*) Pen with brown ink and grey and brown washes; closely incised. 4¾×2¾ in. (12.2×7.1 cm.)   (13468)
The four ovals are inscribed on the ornamental frames 'Saturn & Cybele', 'Coelus & Terra', 'Neptune & . . . (erasure)', and 'Jupiter & Juno'. The engraving, headed 'page 1', completes the third title with 'Amphitrite'.

(*b*) Pencil, pen with brown ink and grey wash over red chalk; incised and reddened at the back. Dimensions as above.
                                    (13470)
The ornamental frames are less complete than those of (*a*); the titles read 'Mercury', 'Venus and her attendants', 'Mars and his attendants', and 'Minerva'. The engraving is headed 'page 87', the inscriptions are the same.

(*c*) Pencil and grey wash over red chalk; incised and reddened at the back. Dimensions as above.   (13469)
The frames are still less complete, being only indicated roughly in pencil and grey wash. The inscriptions read: 'Hercules', 'Bachus and his attend⁵', '. . . (erased) Flora', and 'Pan and his attendants'. The engraving is headed 'page 109' and retains the inscriptions with the mis-spelling.

A paper pasted at the back of the modern mount reads: 'about 15 years since. Sundry Drawings were put into my hands for Sale by Mr. Clee the engraver, of which these 4 are a part, with an assurance they were by Hogarth—Licester [*sic*] Square. Jno. Greenwood. 4th May 1787'. *Anecd.* 1833, p. 400, reads: 'Mr. Lee the engraver' and '4th May 1786'. No engraver of the name Clee is recorded, but there was a sale of the drawings and engravings belonging to Robert Clee at Langford's on the 20th January and following days, 1774 (the only example of the catalogue noted by Lugt was in the Seymour de Ricci collection at Paris).

'Three drawings from King's *Pantheon* and one of a Game at Hazard' formed Lot 136 of the S. Ireland Sale, 1797. They do not, however, reappear at his 1801 sale, where the *Hazard Table* recurs with still another drawing, see on No. 20. The present four drawings are described as in the Royal Collection by *Anecd.* 1833, *loc. cit.* No reference is there made to Samuel Ireland's ownership.

Subject to the question of the date of the edition of King's *Pantheon* where these plates first appeared, the general conception and the handling of the drawings are closely related to the style of Thornhill, and are therefore in no way inconsistent with Hogarth's youthful style. Moreover, they are conceived as ornaments and therefore are related to his work as a silver chaser.

The fourth drawing referred to in Greenwood's note (*supra*) is a medallion showing Minerva with the Gorgon's shield and lightning annihilating a recumbent two-headed and four-armed giant whose lower half terminates in a nine-headed hydra. It differs in scale and handling, and there is no reason to ascribe it to Hogarth (Royal Library 13467).

Fig. 8-10 (Cat. No. 1).   HOGARTH: DESIGNS FOR KING'S 'PANTHEON.'   Royal Library

2. THE LOTTERY, 1721
Plate 1
Royal Library (13481)

Drawing for the engraving in reverse of 1721 (B.M. Sat. 1730, Vol. II, p. 597–8).
Pen and black ink over slight pencil, grey wash; corrections with brown ink and red chalk; incised in places with stylus. Damaged. 9 × 12¾ in. (22.9 × 32.4 cm.)
COLL.: Standly (Sale 1845, Lot 1119 with the print, bought Colnaghi £7).
LIT.: *Anecd.*, 1833, p. 390.

The figure of 'Wantonness' roughly indicated as an afterthought with brown ink over red chalk is taken over into the print, where the figure pulling at the wheel and the grips on it disappear, and the door is opened with the wheel at rest. The purpose evidently is to represent the drawing of the numbers and the prizes as synchronized. A mysterious scrawl drawn on the wheel at the same time as 'Wantonness' does not appear in the print. The capitals and columns of the rostrum have been altered with a ruler and brown ink to form a box base, and the front of the platform has been similarly altered on the right to form panels, both as in the print. Among other points in which the print differs from the drawing it may be noted that cornucopias replace scrolls on the rostrum, 'Fraud' slightly indicated as beckoning from behind a column becomes a head and shoulders emerging from a hatch with open door, and a large snail crawls on the figure of 'Sloth' raising the curtain on the left.
The figures are conceived and drawn much in the manner of Thornhill, and they are largely derivative from older art (*cf.* Antal, *Art Bulletin*, March 1947, p. 38).

3. THE SOUTH SEA BUBBLE, 1721
Plate 2
Royal Library (13479)

Drawing for the engraving, in reverse, of 1721 (B.M. Sat., II, 590 and 591, No. 1722).
Pencil, incised with stylus, rubbed and stained, the corners torn and about one-fifth on the right of the drawing cut off. 8½ × 9¾ in. (21.6 × 24.9 cm.)
COLL.: Standly, Sale 1845, Lot 1250, bought Colnaghi 17s.
LIT.: *Anecd.* 1833, p. 390.

In the print the monument is brought further to the right and the house on the left moved nearer the edge, thus giving more room for a view of St. Paul's, etc., which is not indicated in the drawing. The inn sign with the cat's head is omitted, and the inscription over the door reads 'Raffling for husbands, etc.' where the drawing has 'a ten thousand pound man to be raffled for'. The drawing has no inscription over the merry-go-round, but has on the base of the monument 'This Monument Was'. The figure of Trade is absent from the drawing on the left, as are a goat on the merry-go-round, a Scotsman and the last couple's embrace. The 'balloons' for, or with, legends are all omitted from the print, and the figure of Honesty on the wheel is somewhat softened.
The strong pencil notation over a softer preparation and the already forcible characterization should be remarked. The torture of the wheel is, as noted by Dr. Antal, *l.c.*, p. 38, and older writers, a reminiscence of Callot, while the merry-go-round recalls, perhaps in parody, the gibbet in the same plate (*La Roue*, M. 665).
A portrait of Pope was found by old writers in the small figure in the foreground picking the pocket of a large man. (*Genuine Works*, ii, p. 24.)

4. AN OPERA SINGER (Called Farinelli)
Plate 11
Royal Library (13476)

Pen. 8⅞ × 5⅛ in. (22.6 × 13.1 cm.)

COLL.: Standly, probably Sale 1845, Lot 960, as Senesino, bought Colnaghi £1 10s. 6d.
REPROD.: Etched by Richard Sawyer for Standly, no date; Vasari Soc., Second Series, XV, 1934, No. 5 (Croft-Murray).
EXHIB.: R.A. British Art, 1934, 563 (1104).

This drawing has been generally regarded as related to the print called *Farinelli, Cuzzoni and Senesino performing in Handel's Ptolomeo* (B.M. Sat., II, 625, No. 1768), which is attributed to Hogarth because it is clearly recalled in a banner suspended in his *Burlington Gate* (1724). It is not, however, characteristic of his work and has been ascribed, on the strength of an inscription on one example, to Vanderbank (*Gen. Works*, ii, pp. 39 and 40).
In any case, Farinelli could not be represented in either print since he only came to England ten years later, in 1734. Nor was the opera *Ptolomeo* performed before 1728. It has therefore been argued that the principal male singer represented in the print is Berenstadt, and the opera *Giulio Cesare*, of 1724, and this is confirmed by a version of the print (regarded as a copy by J. Nichols, who alone refers to it, *Biograph. Anecd.*, 1785, p. 139, and *Genuine Works, l.c.*) which mentions, in some doggerel verses engraved below, Berenstadt with Cuzzoni as represented in it. The example complete with the verses in Lord Exeter's Collection has 'Ptolomaeo, Cleopatra and Caesar' written below the characters, another in the British Museum has an erased inscription which, though in a different form, still shows the name Berenstadt, while a third example in the Royal Collection, which has all the inscriptions cut off, has the names Berenstadt, Cuzzoni and Senesino written below the characters. Notwithstanding, therefore, prints in the Royal Collection and at Burghley inscribed with the name 'Farinelli', it cannot be doubted that Berenstadt is one of the singers represented. The description of Farinelli quoted by Nichols (*loc. cit.*) from a pamphlet of 1755 is more likely to have been inspired by the print than to be a confirmation of the traditional identification. The print may well have been revived for Farinelli ten years after its original issue.
Further, a suggestion has recently been made, by Mr. H. Beard to Mr. Croft-Murray, that the incident represented in the print occurs neither in *Ptolomeo* nor *Giulio Cesare* but in Act iii, scene 4, of *Flavio* (1723). In that case, the figure on the left, to which the present drawing bears some resemblance, would not be Berenstadt but Senesino, as is already suggested by the placing of the verses in the example at Burghley and was apparently anticipated by Standly.

The drawing, though bearing a general similarity with the bulky character on the left-hand side of the print and showing much the same attitude, does not emphasize any of the features there caricatured. The free and sketchy handling is inspired by the subject, and no more characteristic of Vanderbank than of Hogarth, little as is known of his drawings at this date. It is noticeable that there appears to be no underlying pencil sketch, and that the drawing, contrary to Hogarth's habit, is in the same direction as the figure in the print.

5-10. DRAWINGS FOR HUDIBRAS, 1726
Royal Library (13459–64)

These six drawings were owned by Samuel Ireland and reproduced by him in *Graph. Illustr.* II, p. 17 *et seq.* Three of them were obtained by him together with Nos. 14–17, the so-called 'Button's Coffee House' drawings from a Mr. Brent, 'an old gentleman who was for many years in habits of intimacy with Hogarth' (*ibid.* I, 25). This may have been about 1781, since the first edition of *Biogr. Anecd.* of that year, in its list of S. Ireland's drawings, mentions (p. 67*) only two of the Hudibras drawings as his, and does not refer to the Coffee House drawings, while the second (1782, p. 126) credits him with five of the Hudibras series and with those which it calls 'Slaughter's Coffee House' drawings (p. 103). In the third edition, 1785, the mistake in the name of the latter is corrected, and the number of Ireland's Hudibras drawings is increased to seven (p. 143).

The present six formed Lot 319 in Ireland's sale, 1801, and were bought (according to *Anecd.*, 1833, p. 390) for £5 15s. by Parker, which is presumably an error for Barker, since the latter's collection was bought by George IV and these six drawings were in 1833 in the Royal Collection.

The further drawing, that for Plate 8 in the series, possessed and reproduced by Ireland, does not figure in either of his sales, but according to *Anecd.*, 1833, *l.c.*, was in the Baring sale, 24th May 1831, where it was bought by Colnaghi £12 1s. 6d., and subsequently in the Standly collection. It was Lot 1087 in the Standly sale (bought by Graves £9 19s. 6d.) and, presumably, was Lot 97 in the Capel Cure Sale 1905, bought by Harvey £15 15s.

Of the remaining five subjects, three were said in *Biogr. Anecd.* 1785 to be in Holland, and two in this country. The latter only are mentioned in *Graph. Illustr.* Drawings of two of the subjects, Plates 5 and 9, in reverse, once in the Robert Mond Collection (Borenius and Wittkower, *Cat.* Nos. 484 and 485), appeared when last seen to be correctly described as copies. They were presumably the two drawings of these subjects exhibited by C. Newton Robinson at Whitechapel (Georgian England), 1906. (See also on No. 11.)

5. HUDIBRAS: THE FRONTISPIECE　　　Plate 4
Royal Library (13459)

Drawing for the engraving, in reverse, pl. 1, of the large set, 1726.

Pencil, with grey-black ink, brown and grey washes; incised. Some green stains as in Nos. 8 and 10 are presumably due to chemicals. $9\frac{1}{2} \times 13\frac{3}{8}$ in. (23.9 × 33.9 cm.)

LIT. AND REPROD.: S. Ireland, *Graphic Illustrations*, Vol. II, p. 20, with aquatint by Rosenberg. *Anecd.* 1833, p. 391.

The drawing has been carefully incised throughout, with the exception of the portrait of Butler, which alone is washed in grey and, though carefully drawn, is not exactly reproduced in the print, and of the polytechnic satyr on the left. This figure is replaced in the print by a Britannia whose mirror, although held up by a laughing faun on her knee, shows her face without satiric distortion. The drawing for this portion was no doubt at one time superimposed, for much of Britannia's spear is drawn with the pen upon the present sheet, either because the added paper was not large enough to contain it, or to mark the precise position where it should be placed (*cf.* No. 76). The slightly drawn tomb of Butler with attendant figures, in the distance right, has been entirely changed in the print. Otherwise the print follows very closely

the careful drawing which is elaborated in delicately toned modelling with the brush after the French manner. Only the garlands around the medallion portrait are left unfinished, being merely indicated with the pencil, but they too are fully incised with the stylus.

6. HUDIBRAS SALLYING FORTH　　　Plate 5
Royal Library (13460)

Drawing for the engraving, in reverse, pl. 2 of the large set, 1726.

Red chalk, with touches of black, and black shading in foreground. Incised. $9\frac{1}{2} \times 13$ in. (24.1 × 32.9 cm.)

LIT. AND REPROD.: As No. 5, the reproduction in *Graphic Illustrations* being in soft-ground etching in sanguine by Le Coeur.

The print differs from the drawing chiefly through the introduction, as indicated in pencil on a trial-proof in the Royal Library, of a house on the right; the peasant's figure is altered, and vegetables on the table and on the ground are omitted. The dog is also altered and retains the same direction as in the drawing. The drawing seems to have been made to some extent with reversal in view, for the buttons on Hudibras' coat are on his left, and both his and Ralpho's swords are on their right. As Hudibras holds his reins in his left hand in the drawing while Ralpho uses his right for this purpose the engraving was bound to be correct in at least one feature, even though the position of Ralpho's hands is changed.

Though fundamentally coarse in its forms the execution is neat and careful with 'tickled' hatching and shading; the foliage and landscape are especially delicate. The dog which is markedly gentle and inoffensive in the drawing is made much more brutal in the print.

7. HUDIBRAS' FIRST ADVENTURE　　　Plate 6
Royal Library (13461)

Drawing for the engraving, in reverse, pl. 3 of the large set, 1726.

Brush drawing in grey, no pencil visible. Incised throughout. $9\frac{1}{2} \times 13\frac{1}{4}$ in. (24.3 × 33.6 cm.)

Damaged and stained before the old mounting, the mount inscribed 'Willm. Hogarth delt.' in S. Ireland's handwriting (the mount identical with that of No. 9).

LIT. AND REPROD.: As No. 5, the reproduction in *Graphic Illustrations* being an aquatint by Rosenberg. *Connoisseur*, XCII, 1933, p. 4.

In the print a pistol is placed in Hudibras' left hand, whereas in the drawing his right hand is clenched. This and the use of left hands for right throughout in the drawing suggest that Hogarth had reversal in view when making it, but overlooked it in his anxiety to introduce the new detail of the pistol.

8. HUDIBRAS AND THE LAWYER　　　Plate 7
Royal Library (13462)

Drawing for the engraving, in reverse, pl. 7 of the large set, 1726.

Pen and brown ink, brown and grey washes, over pencil indications. Some ruling in pen, incised with stylus. The bottom right-hand corner, including the greater part of the dogs, is a restoration. The adjacent parts are stained in green. $9\frac{5}{8} \times 13\frac{1}{4}$ in. (24.8 × 33.7 cm.)

LIT. AND REPROD.: As on No. 5. The aquatint by Merigot.

The print shows several differences of detail, chiefly in the lawyer's throne and the women in the background. The pens in the left hand and buttons show that reversal was kept in mind in the drawing. The drawing is clumsy except for the figures of the two apprentices, and the configuration of the room and throne preposterous; but the actual pen work is vigorous, and anticipates that of the *Industry and Idleness*. The contrast of the two clerks already contains the germ of that series, and both their position and the general conception anticipate the *Paul before Felix*.

9. HUDIBRAS: BURNING THE RUMPS AT TEMPLE BAR
Plate 10
Royal Library (13463)

Drawing for the left-hand portion of the engraving, in reverse, pl. 11 of the large set, 1726.

Pen with brown ink, brown washes, over pencil indications. Incised with the stylus, chiefly in the upper portion where the drawing is sketchy and unfinished. Large tears before mounting (identical with No. 7) seem to show red from chalking at the back. $9\frac{3}{4} \times 8\frac{3}{8}$ in. (24.7×21.2 cm.)

LIT. AND REPROD.: As No. 7.

The drawing was reproduced in *Graphic Illustrations* as complete and was therefore stated in *Anecd.* 1833 to have been perfect when in the possession of Samuel Ireland. Since the old washed mount would appear to be his and must have been made for the drawing in its present state, it is more probable that the reproduction was made up with the help of the engraving.

The bow window with women looking out disappears from the print; otherwise the differences are only minor. Reversal has not been kept in mind. The drawing is spirited throughout, and the figure of the man with the pitchfork well conceived.

10. HUDIBRAS ENCOUNTERS THE SKIMMINGTON
Plate 8
Royal Library (13464)

Drawing for the engraving, in reverse, pl. 12 of the large set, 1726.

Pen with brown ink over pencil and red chalk indications, grey washes in part, heightened with white on brownish paper. Incised with the stylus. Stained with green on the right where, as noticed by S. Ireland, a strip amounting to about one-seventh of the drawing has been cut off. $9\frac{3}{4} \times 17\frac{1}{8}$ in. (24.7×43.4 cm.)

LIT. AND REPROD.: As on No. 5; the aquatint by Merigot.

The chief differences between the drawing and the print are on the left-hand side, where the figure of a man holding a torch has been much improved and reduced; the rider above him is entirely altered. In the centre the figure holding the shirt is changed, as are the horns above it which become those of a cow in the print. The barn loses its two doors in the print. The greater part of the drawing is left at the stage of penwork with, in places, the first flat wash in grey; and several details of the print, as, for example, the head and shoulders of the man holding the bone and cleaver above the bagpiper, are omitted. Probably tracing or pencil work has been obliterated.

Students of Hogarth's psychology will note that two incidents very like those held up for opprobrium in the *First Stage of Cruelty* are present in this subject without any particular note of disapproval; one of them indeed occurred in the now missing part of the drawing, together with an impropriety

which was probably too much for one of its earlier owners. Reversal is kept in mind in the figures of Hudibras and of the mounted egg-thrower; in other figures it has been overlooked.

11. HUDIBRAS ENCOUNTERS THE SKIMMINGTON
Plate 9
Royal Library (13465)

Drawing for the engraving, in reverse, pl. 9 of the small set, 1726.

Pen with brown ink and grey washes over pencil and red chalk, with some incision. Damaged, apparently from folding, and showing signs of red chalk on the back. $5 \times 8\frac{7}{8}$ in. (12.9×22.4 cm.)

COLL.: H. P. Standly (Sale 1845, Lot 1088, with facsimile print; bought Colnaghi £2 2s.).

LIT.: *Anecd.* 1833, p. 392.

Reproduced in aquatint as a facsimile by Richard Sawyer for Standly; private plate.

The 17 illustrations furnished for the small edition of *Hudibras*, 1726, largely followed those of an edition of 1709. In the print the design has been elongated with an extension of the house and several figures have been omitted, while others, including Hudibras himself, have been changed. The result is a considerable loss of vigour and concentration.

The artificiality of the Callot-like shadow figures, more effective in the drawing than in the engraving, is noticeable. It is curious that while the leaping dog in the print is the same as that in the drawing for Plate 2 (No. 6), its counterpart in the present drawing is much nearer the brute in Plate 2 itself, and at the same time Hudibras' nag, which is partly hidden in the present drawing, droops its head towards the dog in the print and is in other respects very like the horse in No. 6. Reversal has been kept in mind.

According to *Anecd.* 1833, p. 392, Standly also possessed a pen-and-ink drawing of *Hudibras, Sidrophel and Whacum*, presumably Lot 1089 in his sale, where it was accompanied by a *Hudibras Sallying Forth*, pen and sepia, also for the octavo edition, and perhaps identical with the drawing described in *Anecd., l.c.*, as that for the print at the top of the proposals for the large edition. Both were bought by Bale for £5 10s. Only one Hudibras drawing is catalogued in the Bale sale May 1881 (Lot 408).

12. THE BEGGARS' OPERA BURLESQUED, 1728
Plate 3
Royal Library (13486)

Drawing for the engraving, in reverse, of *c.* 1728 (anonymous). (B.M. Sat. No. 1807, Vol. II, p. 670.)

Pen with black ink, brown and grey washes, incised. Some touches of pencil, perhaps from tracing, under the heads in the centre; the pencil lines across the sky on each side of the gallows may be due to subsequent accident; red stains on the edges probably come from chalking at the back. $8 \times 9\frac{3}{4}$ in. (20.2×25.1 cm.)

COLL.: Standly (Sale 1845, Lot 894, bought Colnaghi £3 3s.)

LIT.: *Anecd.* 1833, p. 393.

EXHIB.: Spring Gardens (Humour Exhibition), 1885, No. 3. Edinburgh, 1947 (King's Pictures), No. 111.

Except for the insertion of inscriptions there are no important alterations in the print, which, however, is very considerably worked up in detail.

Both pen drawing and washes are lighter, neater and prettier than in previous drawings. They are much in the manner of Gravelot, to whom, or Vandergucht, the print is conjecturally attributed by Nichols & Steevens (*Genuine Works*, ii, 68), the idea borrowed from Coypel in *Les Chats*, Amsterdam, 1728.

13. A CHELSEA PENSIONER, ETC.   Fig. 11

Ascribed to Hogarth   Royal Library (13475)

A Chelsea Pensioner seated on a bench in seven different positions and a young man standing; a profile on another scale. A further figure almost erased.

Pencil, pen and grey wash; two figures and the profile in pencil only; a heavy grey smudge on the face and either several more smudges or a drawing on the reverse (now stuck down). $6\frac{3}{8} \times 11\frac{3}{8}$ in. (16×28.8 cm.)

COLL.: J. Richardson Junior, with mark, Lugt 2170, an unknown mark Lugt 2852. Standly, Sale 1845, Lot 917 (still so inscribed), bought Colnaghi £2 2s.
REPROD.: Facsimile by W. J. Smith for Standly, destroyed 1826 (private plate). (*Anecd.* 1833, p. 291.)

The drawing has been lifted from the old mount and is now stuck down. It is therefore impossible to say whether the attribution to Hogarth goes back to the Richardsons. Further, in the absence of any other similar sketches on the spot by Hogarth on the same scale, it is impossible to speak with any certainty regarding its claims to authenticity on the grounds of style. It seems, however, to be more consistently and ornamentally rounded in its handling, and the limbs, especially the legs, to be on the whole more carefully modelled, than is customary with him. The highly calligraphic loops in the

figure of the standing boy are noticeably foreign to Hogarth's manner.

14. A WAITER AND A HUNGRY CUSTOMER Plate 13
                    British Museum (1861–4–13–506; L.B.24a)

Pen and brown wash. $4\frac{3}{4} \times 5\frac{1}{2}$ in. (12×14 cm.)
Aquatinted by S. Ireland for *Graphic Illustrations*, Vol. I, p. 25 (*cf.* B.M. Sat., Vol. II, No. 1701).
Obtained by S. Ireland about 1781 with the following three drawings and three of the drawings for Hudibras (*cf.* on Nos. 5–10, p. 28) from a Mr. Brent, who was intimate with Hogarth. At Ireland's Sale, 6th May 1797, the four drawings described as 'of characters who frequented Button's Coffee-House', were Lot 137. They were purchased by the Museum at the George Smith Sale, April, 1861. A MS. note, probably in George Smith's hand, with the drawings says 'Harman's Sale'.

Though the identification of the characters in Nos. 14–17 is sufficiently disposed of by L. Binyon in his catalogue, these four drawings and Nos. 18 and 19 in the Royal Library are clearly early (see A. C. Sewter, *Burlington Magazine*, January 1942). There is nothing analogous among Hogarth's drawings to the thick penwork and dark washes of these drawings; but the careful, sensitive treatment of the faces and the awkward, even clumsy, handling of the bodies are paralleled in his early portraits on a small scale, and in the *Hazard Table* (No. 20) which is later. The attitudes are sufficiently caught, but the structure of the body is not grasped. The similarity in the heads of the fat man in Nos. 15–17 and 19 (there called 'Doctor Ward') suggests that the head is either generic or that the drawings have the same personage in view.

Fig. 11 (Cat. No. 13).   ASCRIBED TO HOGARTH: A CHELSEA PENSIONER. Royal Library

15. EXAMINING A WATCH   Plate 18
British Museum (1861–4–13–508; L.B. 24b)

Pen and brown wash. 5 × 7⅜ in. (12.7 × 18.7 cm.)
Aquatinted by S. Ireland, *loc. cit.*, p. 31.
See on No. 14. The younger man should be compared both in features and in dress with the man in the centre of the *Hazard Table* (No. 20).

16. DRAUGHT PLAYERS INTERRUPTED   Plate 16
British Museum (1861–4–13–509; L.B. 25a)

Pen and brown wash. 5 × 7 in. (12.7 × 17.8 cm.)
Aquatinted by S. Ireland, *loc. cit.*, p. 34.

Though this drawing and No. 17 have been given different titles, they are evidently two drafts of the same scene with one of the characters wearing a hat, two others transposed and slightly altered in feature and only the fourth materially changed, and, even so, bearing a strong family resemblance. The chairs and the table are the same, even to the lack of legs, a feature which the table shares with personages in both drawings. The main idea and some of the details seem to occur, with more freedom, in the enigmatic oil sketch, engraved as after Hogarth and called the *Debates on Palmistry* (*cf* A. C. Sewter, *l.c.*)

17. A GAME OF DRAUGHTS ENDED   Plate 17
British Museum (1861–4–13–507; L.B. 25b)

Pen and brown wash. 5 × 7⅜ in. (12.7 × 18.7 cm.)
Aquatinted by S. Ireland, *loc. cit.*, p. 38.   See on No. 16.

18. TWO PAIRS OF FIGURES CALLED 'DESIGN FOR THE HAPPY MARRIAGE' AND 'FIRST DESIGN FOR THE DOCTORS IN THE HARLOT'S PROGRESS'   Plate 14
Royal Library (13478)

Pen and brown wash over pencil indications, inscribed 'Hogarth' in a later hand. 5⅛ × 6⅞ in. (13.2 × 17.5 cm.)
COLL.: Standly, Sale 1845, Lot 1022, bought by Colnaghi, £3 13s. 6d.
REPROD.: W. J. Smith, private plates (two) for Standly destroyed 1825. (B.M. Sat., 1985; *cf. Anecd.* 1833, pp. 292 and 394.)
EXHIB.: R.A. British Art, 1934, 564 (1120).

These drawings are nearer than No. 19 to the 'Button's Coffee House' drawings, and are almost equally clumsy. The traditional connection of the pair on the left hand with what is known of the *Happy Marriage* projects, and that of the two male figures with the doctors in Plate 5 of the *Harlot's Progress*, are very remote, though it is possible that some memory of this pair of gently disputing doctors was in Hogarth's mind when he conceived the violently agitated couple in that scene. At any rate he could scarcely have returned to these figures after painting the picture. The sheet may accordingly be dated well before 1731, when the *Harlot's Progress* series was painted. On the other hand, the intention of the two figures on the left appears to be entirely different from that of the chief couple in the print by Ryder after the sketch for Scene 3 of the *Happy Marriage* (*Graphic Illustrations*, II, 128). Here there is every indication of an improper proposal, or at any rate an intrigue; in the picture the lady is in the act of relieving one of the 'indigent' or accepting his thanks. A somewhat nearer parallel might be found either in the principal figures in the late

picture *The Masqueraders* (also lost, engraved by T. Cook, 1805) or indeed in the *Laughing Audience* of 1733.

19. DR. MISAUBIN AND DR. WARD   Plate 15
Royal Library (13472)

Pencil, pen and brown ink, brown wash. Inscribed under the figures 'Dr. Misaubin and Dr. Ward' in a later hand. 4 × 6 in. (10.2 × 15.4 cm.)
COLL.: According to *Anecd.* 1833, pp. 292 and 394, where this drawing appears to be confused with No. 18, 'these two small heads were bought at Baker's Sale and are in Mr. Standly's possession'. It is not traceable in the catalogue of the George Baker Sale, Sotheby's, 16th June 1825. At Standly's Sale, 1845, it was Lot 1152, bought by Colnaghi £2 15s.
REPROD.: W. J. Smith, private plate destroyed 1827, for Standly. (B.M. Sat., Div. I, Vol. II, No. 1986.) Richard Sawyer, aquatint, 1828.
EXHIB.: Royal Institute (English Humourists), 1889, No. 2.

This drawing is more competent than the 'Button's Coffee House' drawings, but it and the preceding drawing are akin to them in the soft and unusually unbroken pen line, and the care in shaping the contours. The contrast of fat and lean characters recurs there and in Plate 5 of the *Harlot's Progress*, with which the personages supposed to be represented here are traditionally related, but may be disregarded as a commonplace.

20. HAZARD TABLE   Plate 19
Royal Library (13474)

Pen with grey ink, grey wash. 8⅞ × 12⅞ in. (22.6 × 32.6 cm.)
COLL.: Samuel Ireland, Sale 1797, Lot 136 with No. 1, and Sale 1801, Lot 311 with *Swearing a Bastard Child*, 11s. Mentioned as in the Royal Collection *Anecd.* 1833, p. 403, see No. 102 *infra*.
REPROD.: *Graph. Illustr.*, ii, p. 104. Aquatint by Le Coeur. *Connoisseur*, XCII, 1933, p. 5, pl. 3.
EXHIB.: R.I. (English Humourists), 1889. No. 2. Spring Gardens (Humour Exhibition), 1925, No. 1.

Samuel Ireland failed to 'recognize in this drawing the faintest traces of that characteristic humour on which the reputation of Hogarth is so justly founded', and he saw 'something so lifeless and inanimate in their countenances' that the personages might be 'an assembly of gossips sitting round the tea-table' rather than dice players. Presumably, since he accepted the identification of the youth with the Garter as Frederick Prince of Wales, he expected from Hogarth some violent satire against both Royalty and gaming such as in his day Gillray and Rowlandson were producing. On the contrary, Hogarth consistently sought for Royal patronage; the figure of the prelate is entirely in his manner, and the lack of animation or even of concentration of glances in the other personages is a common feature in his portrait groups. The drawing is more carefully executed than, but is related to, the 'Button's Coffee House' groups.

The subject of the drawing is by no means easy to explain, and it bears a distinct relation to a painting by Mercier lately in the possession of Messrs. Tooth, and probably once in the Northwick Collection as by Hogarth. There, too, a tutor is apparently debauching his pupils at the hazard table. A still further problem is introduced if the identification is accepted of the youth with the Garter as Frederick Prince of Wales, since the boy here would clearly appear to be under 21, whereas the Prince of Wales was born on 20th January 1706–7, and only came to England on the 3rd December

1728, when he was nearly 22. According to the *Free and Impartial Reflexions on the Character, Life and Death of Frederick, Prince of Wales* (Philobiblon Soc. Misc. vii, 1862-3, p. 4): 'Of the capacity and talents of his Governors and Tutors nothing has been particularly mentioned'. If, on the other hand, the drawing could be placed after 1751, George III as Prince of Wales might be intended.

21. AN ILLUSTRATION FOR A NOVEL: A DUEL SCENE   Fig. 12
Ascribed to Hogarth.

British Museum (1858–4–17–619; L.B. 26b)

Pen and grey wash. $7\frac{1}{4} \times 3\frac{7}{8}$ in. (18.4×9.8 cm.)

Some lines of the text illustrated are written in the margin below, and cut off on both sides.

Acquired in 1858 with Nos. 82 and 85.

The handwriting may be Hogarth's; the conception and

Fig. 12 (Cat. No. 21). ASCRIBED TO HOGARTH: AN ILLUSTRATION FOR A NOVEL—A DUEL SCENE. British Museum

execution have not sufficient character to permit either affirmation or denial of his authorship. If the drawing is his it must date from about the time, 1731, of his illustration to Molière's *Avare* (No. 101). It should be noted that, unlike that drawing, the present design is not made for reversal, a point which is generally observed in Hogarth's drawings for prints, strangely indifferent though he was to the reversal of his paintings in the prints from them.

The drawing does not correspond in size with the indian ink drawing of a duel mentioned in *Anecd.* 1833, p. 405, as in Standly's Collection, formerly Udny's, nor is Windsor Castle visible in the background.

22. BOYS PEEPING AT NATURE, 1731   Plate 12
Royal Library (13497)

Drawing for the engraving (B.M. Sat., 1943) in reverse, used for the subscription ticket for the *Harlot's Progress*, 1731. Pencil and grey wash, touched with pen and black ink; incised in places; additions in pencil, within ruled pencil border. $4 \times 5\frac{1}{4}$ in. (10.2×13.3 cm.)

COLL.: The drawing appears to have been unknown to S. Ireland, and Richard Livesay, who only reproduce the first state of the plate.

Standly, Sale 1845, Lot 1025, bought Colnaghi £1. As the drawing is not mentioned in *Anecd.* 1833, presumably Standly acquired it after that date.

The drawing is very neatly executed with shading and hatching in fine brushwork. It has reversal in view and is exactly followed in the print except that the wall is carried to the top of the plate, and a Latin inscription inserted. Pencil afterthoughts in the top left-hand corner of the drawing, a palette and a medallion, are not carried into the print.

As is noted by Dr. Antal, *l.c.*, p. 39, the many-bosomed torso of Nature is taken by Hogarth from the picture by Rubens which belonged to Thornhill. It is repeated in the *Foundling Hospital Arms* (No. 66). The idea of *amorini* practising with the utensils of the arts occurs so frequently that it seems idle to enquire whence Hogarth may have derived it. There are compositions of this subject in Thornhill's sketchbook at the British Museum (L.B. 68, *f.* 38). It is, however, possible that Hogarth had in mind and was actually parodying the title-page of a drawing-book after Nicolas Poussin (published by Veuve Poilly, *n.d.*, reproduced in L. Coutil, *N. Poussin*, 1904, No. 3, fig. 3), in which at least two of the figures are in similar attitudes, and the Hogarthian mind might have seen a similar indiscreet observation of a statue. The removal in later states of the print of this incident in the interest of propriety deprived, but with no great loss, his idea of all meaning. It, however, gave him an opportunity of paying homage to Thornhill by scheming out, on Thornhill's lines, a portrait head on the canvas which takes the place of the satyr.

23. SCENE IN *THE BEGGARS' OPERA*   Plate 20
Royal Library (13487)

Black chalk with touches of white on the same dark blue paper as Nos. 24 and 28; the outlines of the chief figures pricked; splashed with oil colour. $14\frac{5}{8} \times 19\frac{3}{8}$ in. (37.3×49.2 cm.)

COLL.: S. Ireland Sale, 1797, Lot 134; 1801, Lot 308, with *Falstaff* (*cf.* No. 24): 'large sketches in chalk from Hogarth's Sketchbook purchased by Mr. Ireland from Mrs. Lewis', 8s. 6d. According to *Anecd.* 1833, p. 401 in the Royal Collection by 1833. Another *Beggars' Opera*, black and white chalk, was in the Standly Sale, Lot 1308, bought Tiffin, 8s.

EXHIB.: Grosvenor Gallery, 1877, No. 1007; R.I. (English Humourists), 1889, No. 2.

S. Ireland, *Graphic Illustrations*, I, 59, states that the drawing was a preparation for either the Duke of Leeds' picture (engraved by William Blake in 1790), or the duplicate painted for Sir Henry Gough; his wording is not clear. It is not the sketch for the Duke of Leeds' picture, nor for the duplicate of it painted for Sir Archibald Grant about 1731 and now in the Tate Gallery, if the pedigree given in the catalogue for it is correct. In both these versions, while the general disposition is the same as in the present drawing, Lucy, on the left, is nearer to Macheath and the attitudes of three of the other figures are different. The arrangement and attitudes shown in the drawing are, however, followed in a third version, the Huth and Carysfort picture now in the possession of Colonel the Hon. J. J. Astor (reproduced in Christie's catalogue, 18th March 1921). This corresponds to the Gough picture which, according to *Biogr. Anecd.* 1785, p. 23, was not painted for Sir Henry Gough, but bought by him from Sir William Saunderson. The lightly sketched background figures in the drawing differ from both the Leeds-Tate Gallery and the Huth versions. The drawing seems also to have been followed in the undated popular print, in reverse, by J. Sympson after Hogarth, *The Ticket for the Benefit of Mr. Walker*. The poses in the drawing are easier and the composition more flowing than in the Leeds-Tate Gallery version, and the handling is free and masterly, if the figures show some disproportion and uncertainty in their spatial relationship.

The different versions of the picture are reproduced in the *Burlington Magazine*, June 1948, by Mr. R. B. Beckett, whose opinion that the 'Huth' version is the earlier was arrived at independently of the drawing and is strongly confirmed by it. The drawing can be safely dated between 1728 and 1731, and this probably fixes also the other drawings from 'Hogarth's Sketch-book'.

24. FALSTAFF EXAMINING HIS RECRUITS Plate 21
Royal Library (13491)

Black and white chalk on the same dark blue paper as Nos. 23 and 29. 15⅝ × 21¼ in. (38.9 × 54 cm.)

COLL.: See on No. 23.

LIT.: *Anecd.* 1833, p. 402, where the drawing then in the Royal Collection was stated to have been in the possession of S. Ireland in 1782. S. Ireland does not mention this drawing though he reproduces (*Graphic Illustrations* II, 72) a picture (described in 1809 as a sketch. *Gen. Works*, iii, 304) then in the possession of Mrs. Garrick and now of Lord Iveagh. His print shows all the figures of the picture in approximately the same attitudes and arrangemer.t as in the drawing, with the exception that an additional head is inserted in the background on the right. The drawing shows none of the accessory detail, nor is the architecture indicated, but the whole story is fully told. In handling, the drawing is much swifter and less rounded than in the *Beggars' Opera*. The white chalk already marks the principal lights.

25. NUDE FEMALE ACADEMY FIGURE (before 1736).
Plate 22
Royal Library (13482)

Black and white chalk within ruled lines on brown paper,

rubbed and slightly stained with oil. 14⅝ × 11¼ in. (37.3 × 28.7 cm.)

Inscribed within the ruled margin at foot, in almost erased pencil: 'From Hogarth's Sketch Book', and in ink, below: 'The original Sketch from the life for the principal female figure in the picture of the Pool of Bethesda at St. Bartholomew's Hospital—by William Hogarth—this figure was drawn in St. Martins lane—and given to me by Chs. Catton Esqre. Nov. 21 1794. S.I.'

COLL.: Perhaps one of the three sketches of academy figures forming Lot 135 in S. Ireland's Sale, 6th May 1797, and Lot 307 of his sale May 1801 (see on No. 27). In the Royal Library before 1833.

LIT.: *Anecd.* 1833, p. 394, which inserts (presumably from *Gen. Works* ii, 190) into the inscription after 'St. Martins lane', '. . . and is said to have represented Nell Robinson, a celebrated courtezan and the drawing was' and reads, 'Cotton.'

The drawing, though beyond reasonable doubt used for the principal female figure in the *Pool of Bethesda* (1736), has every appearance of a drawing made from the model in the life school and then found suitable for use in the picture, rather than of a study made specially for the purpose.

Fig. 13 (*cf.* on Cat. No. 25).   ASCRIBED TO HOGARTH
NUDE FEMALE FIGURE.   Pierpont Morgan Library

A study of a nude female figure half-reclining (fig. 13), in the Pierpont Morgan Library (III, 32g, black chalk, heightened with white on grey paper, 16¾×10½ in.; from the Fairfax Murray Collection) will shortly be published, it is understood, by Dr. Edgar Wind as a study by Hogarth for his lost picture of *Danae*. There is a tower in the background but, so far as can be judged from a photograph, the drawing appears to be too accomplished and the modelling too soft to accord with Hogarth's life-studies, and the attitude of pensive relaxation is scarcely suggestive of Danae.

26. HYMEN   Plate 23

The Marquess of Exeter

Black chalk on buff paper, folded horizontally. 19¾×14½ in. (50×37 cm.)

Drawing used for the ticket 'Hymen and Cupid' for the *Masque of Alfred*, performed at Cliveden House on the Princess Augusta's birthday, 11th August 1748, and afterwards intended as a ticket for a raffle for *Sigismunda*. (*Biogr. Anecd.* 1781, p. 142. *Anecd.* 1833, p. 225.)

The drawing is included in the ninth Earl of Exeter's manuscript list, 1782, as (?) 'Genie with the Lute'. In the book of engravings from which it has been taken, the print is described as the 'ticket for yᵉ mask of Alfred which was exhibited in yᵉ gardens at Clifden on yᵉ 12 (illeg.) yᵉ Lady Augusta now Princess of Brunswick's birthday when Barberini & all yᵉ opera dancers & singers performd & yᵉ Principal English with yᵉ foreign Ministers being invited, the Fete lasted 5 nights'. The drawing appears to have been vaguely known to Austin Dobson (*ed.* 1907, p. 251).

The drawing is closely followed in the engraving (fig. 14) except for the turn of the head and the drapery. It may therefore have been made as a study for the special purpose, but the use of Thornhill's formula for placing the features of the face suggests an earlier date and an academic study made in St. Martin's Lane such as Nos. 25 and 28. The lute and torch have been lightly superimposed. *A priori* it seems unlikely that Hogarth would have had recourse to the model for so trite a figure as this, and for so occasional a purpose.

It is clear from Lord Exeter's manuscript list and from his

Fig. 14 (cf. on Cat. No. 26).   HOGARTH: HYMEN AND CUPID.
1748.   Engraving

note against a space which is now blank in his book of engravings that he possessed the original drawing for the other and better-known subscription ticket for *Sigismunda*, 'Time smoking a picture'. It is now no longer in any of the volumes, nor is it entered on the list drawn up by the British Museum of the drawings mounted by them.

27. THREE FIGURES   Fig. 15

Royal Library (13489)

A woman standing between a bearded sitting figure in oriental robes and an old woman.

Black and white chalk on deep blue paper. 12⅝×11 in. (32.3×28 cm.)

Fig. 15 (Cat. No. 27).   HOGARTH: THREE FIGURES.
Royal Library

LIT. and COLL.: *Anecd.* 1833, p. 402, describes this as 'a beautiful female, placed between a Jewish Elder and an old woman, "from Hogarth's sketchbook"' and in the Royal Collection. The inverted commas, together with the character of the drawing, suggest an identification with Lot 307 in S. Ireland's Sale, 1801: 'three, Susanna and the Elders, in chalk taken from Hogarth's sketchbook', as was Lot 308, also in this collection (Nos. 23 and 24).

28. A NUDE MALE ACADEMY FIGURE HOLDING A JAVELIN   Plate 24

Royal Library (13488)

Black chalk heightened with white and touched with red, on deep blue paper. 21½×15¾ in. (54.5×40 cm.)

Presumably identical with the academical study of a whole-length naked figure in chalk on blue paper in the Royal Collection mentioned in *Anecd.* 1833, p. 402, and perhaps forming one of the three drawings from Hogarth's sketchbook, Lot 307, in S. Ireland's Sale 1801, and the three sketches of Academy figures, Lot 135 in his sale in 1797 (see on No. 27).

To be compared with No. 84 (Plate 25).

29. HOGARTH'S TOUR, 1732

British Museum (1847–3–20–1—9)

Nine drawings, two being entirely by Scott, illustrating a manuscript account of a 'five-days' peregrination' or 'five-days' tour by land and water', from London into Kent, taken in May 1732 by Hogarth with Samuel Scott the artist, the younger Thornhill, Ebenezer Forrest, a notary and William Tothall, woollen-draper, smuggler and shell-collector. The journal was written by Forrest, Hogarth and Scott made the drawings which were pasted on the opposite pages, and Thornhill provided a map. According to *Biographical Anecdotes* 1781, p. 68*, the book was produced, bound, gilt and lettered, and read at the Bedford Coffee House on the second night after their return. As the manuscript is most carefully written and the drawings adorned with gold and washed borders, this seems remarkably quick work. The book was in the possession of Theodosius Forrest in 1781, from whom it passed to his executor, Peter Coxe, and it was acquired by the British Museum in 1847 from Messrs. Graves. A facsimile of the drawings was published with the journal by Richard Livesay in 1781, the first states of the plates in outline and hand-coloured, the final aquatinted. The suggestion hazarded by the present writer in 1924 that Rowlandson assisted in the etching (*Thomas Rowlandson*, p. 14) has recently been confirmed by the copy of both manuscript and illustrations in Rowlandson's hand acquired by the British Museum.

Plate 26

(*a*) Frontispiece: *Mr. Somebody*. Emblematic, according to Livesay, of 'a short tour by land and water, backwards and forwards, without head or tail'. Broad pen, with brown ink and brown wash over pencil, and watercolour. Signed 'W.H.' at foot, right. $7\frac{7}{8} \times 12$ in. (20 × 30.3 cm.)

Plate 27

(*b*) *Upnor Castle*, with Scott sketching and Hogarth pointing. Pen with brown ink and watercolour. The manuscript suggests that the castle was drawn by Hogarth and the shipping by Scott, but it may mean that two separate drawings were made. Apparently on this assumption the drawing has been credited entirely to Hogarth, but if, as is most probable, there was once a pencil foundation, the shipping, which is more careful than the rest, may have been by Scott.
Inscribed below: 'A. Upnor Castle. B. The Medway. C. Mr. Thornhill. D. Mr. Hogarth. E. Mr. Forrest. F. Mr. Tothall. G. Mr. Scott'. $8\frac{3}{8} \times 12$ in. (21.4 × 30.3 cm.)

Plate 28

(*c*) *Breakfast at the Nag's Head*. Pen with brown ink and grey wash over pencil, and watercolour. $8\frac{1}{8} \times 12\frac{5}{8}$ in. (20.5 × 32 cm.)
Inscribed below: 'A. The Fisherman Shaving. B. Mr. Thornhill. C. Mr. Tothall Shaving Himself. D. Mr. Hogarth Drawing this Drawing. E. Mr. Forrest at Breakfast. F. Mr. Scott Finishing a Drawing'.
Reproduced (colour) A.D. 1902, opp. p. 38.

Plate 29

(*d*) *The Embarkation for Sheerness*. By Hogarth and Scott. Pen and watercolour; probably the figures only, in stronger pen and brown ink, by Hogarth. $8 \times 12\frac{5}{8}$ in. (20.4 × 32 cm.)
Inscribed below: 'A. The Boat. B. Mr. Tothall at the Helm. C. Mr. Thornhill Lending a Hand. D. Mr. Hogarth. E. Mr. Forrest Pushing Forward. F. Mr. Scott. G. Sheerness'.

Plate 30

(*e*) *Queenborough*. Pen with black ink and grey wash over slight pencil. The manuscript mentions Hogarth as taking a sketch in the town; he would seem to have used Scott's materials for the purpose, then or later.
$8\frac{1}{8} \times 12\frac{3}{8}$ in. (20.5 × 31.5 cm.)
Inscribed below: 'A. The Town of Queenborough. B. The Clockhouse. C. Mr. Forrest. D. Mr. Hogarth with the E. Sailors. F. The Church'.

Plate 31

(*f*) *Tomb of Lord Shorland in Minster Church*. Broad pen with brown ink over pencil, grey wash. $7\frac{7}{8} \times 12\frac{1}{2}$ in. (22.6 × 31.8 cm.)

Plate 32

(*g*) Tailpiece: *Mr. Nobody*. Pen with brown ink over pencil, and watercolour. Drawn below the signatures on the paper of the last page of the book. Initials 'W.H.' at foot, right.

30. GABRIEL HUNT   Plate 34

The Marquess of Exeter

Brush and grey wash on two pieces of white paper joined horizontally and stuck down on a very thin panel. Much faded and damaged. $10\frac{1}{2} \times 7\frac{1}{8}$ in. (26.5 × 18 cm.)
A note in the ninth Earl of Exeter's handwriting on a separate slip reads: 'The original drawing of Mr. Gabriel Hunt given to Lord Exeter Nov. 21st 1782 by Mr. Forrest'. For the entry in his manuscript list and for Livesay's note see on No. 88. See also the further references there quoted.
Lord Exeter's note on this drawing reads, probably following *Biogr. Anecd.* 1782, p. 106, or 1785, p. 411: 'The drawing from which this print was taken Hogarth did at the time the Club was held at the Bedford Arms Tavern in Covent Garden about the year 1733, the Hanger placed in his buttonhole characterizes that Period when the public streets were so infested with robbers that it was dangerous for any Gentleman to walk home late at night without being armd.'

31(*a*). THE CALVES' HEAD CLUB, 1735   Fig. 16a

Ascribed to Hogarth.   Royal Library (13484)

Drawing for the engraving (by Vandergucht), in reverse, [1735] (B.M. Sat., 2141 and 2142).
Pencil and grey wash; closely incised, within a ruled border. $7\frac{1}{4} \times 7\frac{7}{8}$ in. (18.3 × 20 cm.)
Inscribed in pen in the margin, at top: 'The true Effigies of the Members of the Calves'-head Club', and at foot, in S. Ireland's handwriting: 'This drawing was given to me May 9 1781 by Mr. Van der Guhct [*sic*]—(whose Father engrav'd it) as an original drawing of Hogarth's'.
COLL.: S. Ireland (not specified in sales). Standly, Sale 1845, Lot 911, bought Colnaghi £3 13s. 6d., with the following.
LIT.: *Anecd.* 1833, p. 394.

The design, as well as the execution of the print, was attributed by John Ireland (*Hogarth Illustrated*, Vol. III, p. 375) to Vandergucht.
A note in Horace Walpole's hand on his copy of the print, now in the B.M., repeats the statement of the inscription on the drawing. The drawing is followed closely by the print, a picture of the execution of King Charles hanging on the wall becoming more detailed. Reversal is intended in the principal figure but forgotten elsewhere. Even more than in No. 33 (*Tartuff's Banquet*) the dainty forms throughout and the neat execution seem inconsistent with Hogarth's authorship, while

The True Effigie of the Members of The Calves head Club

This drawing was given to me May 9. 1781. by Mr. Vander Gucht (whose Father engrav'd it) as an original drawing of Hogarths.

Fig. 16a (Cat. No. 31a).   ASCRIBED TO HOGARTH: THE CALVES' HEAD CLUB.
Royal Library

Fig. 16b (Cat. No. 31b).   ASCRIBED TO
HOGARTH: THE CALF'S HEAD.
Royal Library

the weakness in the shadowed objects in the foreground is entirely foreign to his manner.

31(b). THE SAME; THE CALF'S HEAD ONLY

Fig. 16b

Ascribed to Hogarth.   Royal Library (13483)

Pencil. $3\frac{1}{2} \times 4\frac{5}{8}$ in. (9×11.7 cm.)

COLL.: With the preceding, in Standly's Sale, Lot 911.

The head only, without the platter, but with the tufts of hair which appear in the print and may have been intended to enhance the reference to Charles I.

Though stronger than the reduced version, this drawing contains nothing which definitely points to Hogarth as its author.

32. A GARRET SCENE (? Hogarth)   Fig. 17

British Museum (Z–1–3)

Red chalk, squared in black; some alterations in black. Ruled red border with a ruled black vertical border within it, the squaring connected with the latter. Words and numbers in red chalk 'in full' (repeated and erased), 'by 16' and '$13\frac{5}{8}$' and some pencil sketches of clearly later date on the reverse. $9\frac{1}{2} \times 13$ in. (24×33 cm.) without margins.

Inscribed 'Aristot on F.' on the book.

This drawing, acquired by the British Museum before 1837, remained unmounted perhaps owing to its distasteful character, until Mr. Croft-Murray recognized it as probably the work of Hogarth, with a possibility that it might be the earliest idea in the *Harlot's Progress* series. This seems on the whole unlikely; but the Hogarthian character of the drawing is pronounced and is clearer in the original red chalk

than in the reproduction. The attendant or 'bunter', as Vertue calls her counterpart in the third plate of the *Harlot's Progress*, is entirely in Hogarth's vein. The precise and detailed work is paralleled in the second drawing of the Hudibras series (No. 6), while the cat and the arrangement of the foreground objects are characteristic of him, more especially in the pencilled alteration on the right. This alteration was necessitated by the reduction of the drawing on that side as shown by the black rules line on the inner side of the original margin. The size as altered would not correspond with that of the *Industry and Idleness* series and it is much below that of the *Harlot's Progress*. There would, moreover, appear to be no place for the subject in either series, and Hogarth's predilection for bedside scenes, with or without disease, was so marked that it seems superfluous to enquire further into the purpose of this drawing.

33. TARTUFF'S BANQUET   Fig. 18

Ascribed to Hogarth.   Royal Library (13473)

Drawing for the anonymous engraving, in reverse, of 1736/7 entitled 'Tartuff's Banquet'. (B.M. Sat., 2281.)

Pencil and yellow-brown wash over red chalk indications; closely incised; within a ruled border. $7\frac{7}{8} \times 9\frac{1}{8}$ in. (19.9×23.2 cm.) with border.

Inscribed in the margin below in pencil and in different hands 'Orator Henley' and 'by Hogarth'.

COLL.: Standly, 1845, Lot 1263 bought Colnaghi £4 6s.

LIT.: *Anecd.* 1833, p. 403; *A.D.*, 1907, p. 243.

REPROD.: Aquatint by William J. Smith for Standly, private plate, destroyed 1827.

The drawing throws no light on the question whether Orator

Fig. 17 (Cat. No. 32). (?) HOGARTH: A GARRET SCENE. British Museum

Henley or, as is more probable, Dr. Gibson, Bishop of London, is represented. Tartuff's head is said further, by Nichols (*Gen. Works*, iii, 331), to resemble Dean Swift's. The print is generally attributed to Vandergucht, and the drawing

Fig. 18 (Cat. No. 33). ASCRIBED TO HOGARTH (? BY VANDERGUCHT): TARTUFF'S BANQUET. Royal Library

with its meticulous precision (closely followed in the incision) and attenuated forms is not characteristic of Hogarth. Probably the most Hogarthian detail is the performance of the pug-dog in the right-hand bottom corner, but the subtlety with which an additional comic effect is obtained in the engraving by leaving the monk's head turned in the original direction while all the rest of the drawing is reversed, is somewhat inconsistent with his robust humour.

34. DON QUIXOTE RELEASES THE GALLEY-
        SLAVES (Book III, Chapter viii).   Plate 35
                                        Royal Library (13471)
Drawing for the engraving, in reverse, intended for Lord Carteret's edition of *Don Quixote*, 1738, not used, but issued subsequently as the sixth of Hogarth's eight plates.
Pen with black ink and grey washes within a ruled border; roughly incised in places. With border 9⅜×7⅜ in. (23.7 × 18.9 cm.).
COLL.: Standly, Sale 1845, Lot 935 bought Colnaghi 25s.
LIT.: *Anecd.* 1833, p. 395.
REPROD.: Cundall, *Connoisseur*, XCII, 1933, p. 5.

Except for Don Quixote's helmet, his horse's foreleg, the broken fetter on the slave's outstretched hand and a gun on the ground, the print follows the drawing very closely. No regard has been paid to the need for reversal. Though coarsely washed and touched with the brush, the pen drawing is highly careful, even elegant, no doubt in emulation of Coypel.

The drawing for *Sancho's Feast*, which was engraved separately in 1733 and revised for inclusion in this series (*Anecd.* 1833, p. 207), was reproduced in facsimile by S. Ireland, *Graph. Illus.*, ii, p. 32, and twice (by Sawyer and Lewis) for its later possessor, Standly. It was Lot 1226, bought Graves £15 15s., in his sale, and probably Capel-Cure, Sale, 1905, Lot 94 with facsimiles, bought Maggs, £6 5s. and C. Newton Robinson, Christie's, 6th April 1914, Lot 19, bought Paterson £19 19s.

35. DON QUIXOTE: THE CURATE AND BARBER DISGUISING THEMSELVES (Book III, Chapter xiii.) Fig. 19
Royal Library (13490)

Drawing for the engraving, in reverse, intended for Lord Carteret's edition of *Don Quixote* (1738), not used, but issued subsequently as the last of Hogarth's eight plates.
Black chalk on blue paper, reinforced with pen and white chalk, in ruled border, black over red. Incised. Rubbed and stained. With border 10 × 7⅝ in. (25.4 × 19.4 cm.)
COLL.: Standly, Sale 1845, Lot 934, bought Colnaghi 10s.
LIT.: *Anecd.* 1833, p. 395.

An almost illegible pencil inscription in the margin at foot may read as on the print and given above.

The differences from the print are very slight, e.g. rafters are shown in the drawing and a hat on the heap of clothes at the foot, while a jug on the shelf and a scutcheon on the wall which are in the print are absent in the drawing. The drawing

is so much rubbed and discoloured that it is impossible to say how much of its weakness is due to Hogarth.

36. THE PILGRIMS AT CUMBERS Plate 36
Pierpont Morgan Library, iii, 31

Pencil. Inscribed in the margin below with the title as given and 'Vol. I, page 9'. 'July 20 1740'. 'W.H. fect' and, in ink, the name Hogarth in a later hand, probably Esdaile's. 8⅜ × 10 in. (21.3 × 25.4 cm.)
COLL.: Esdaile (with mark, but not traceable in the sale catalogues), Joly and Fairfax Murray. Presumably Lot 1306 of the Standly sale, 1845, with the title and date 'a very spirited drawing in pencil', bought by Graves 11s.
REPROD.: Pierpont Morgan Library III, 31.
Nothing is known of Cumbers nor of the occasion represented.

Fig. 20 (Cat. No. 37).   AFTER HOGARTH:
SIMON LORD LOVAT.   British Museum

37. SIMON LORD LOVAT Fig. 20
After Hogarth. British Museum (1893–5–16–390. L.B.22)

Head and shoulders, full face, turned slightly left. Black and white chalk with stump or black wash on coarse brown paper. 10⅛ × 8¼ in. (25.7 × 21 cm.)
Acquired in 1893 from the Fine Art Society.

The weakness of this drawing, which cannot be entirely accounted for by its condition, proclaims it to be a copy from a painting, probably the portrait acquired by the National Portrait Gallery in 1866, which is approximately the same size. This is indicated also by the white chalk line which is not confined to high lights, but marks all the contours and even surrounds the tie which is abbreviated and somewhat more

Fig. 19 (Cat. No. 35).   HOGARTH: DON QUIXOTE—THE CURATE AND THE BARBER DISGUISING THEMSELVES.   Royal Library

splayed than in the painting, no doubt because of the reduction to a head and shoulders only. This is, perhaps, the drawing sold as Lot 1121 at the Standly Sale as 'Lord Lovat, a drawing in chalk of the head by J. Ireland' (bought by Graves 9s.), perhaps exhibited R.A. 1879, No. 335 by Jeffery Whitehead.

The drawing is in the same direction as Hogarth's etching of 25 August 1746 (*B.M. Sat.*, III, Pt. I, p. 608, No. 2801). In it the action, as is noted in *B.M. Sat.*, is left-handed, since the normal method of counting with the fingers is to use the right hand on the left. The buttons on the coat are also on the wrong side. *B.M. Sat.* accordingly supposes that the print reverses, as usual, the action in the picture at the National Portrait Gallery. This is not the case. The portrait at the N.P.G. is also left-handed, both in the action of the hands and in the buttons of the coat. Either, therefore, Hogarth in painting that picture made use of his print rather than of his original drawing as being more elaborated, or it is a copy by another hand from the print.

Another version of the same portrait has the figure in the right direction, i.e. showing the buttons on the right hand side and the right hand used in counting. It is represented by a drawing in pen and wash in the possession of Lord Saltoun and reproduced by A. Fraser (Lord Saltoun), *The Frasers of Philorth*, 1879, vol. II, opp. p. 180. This shows Lord Lovat in the same position but with a different table, which has differently inscribed books upon it, the shadow of prison bars on the wall, left, and, in the left-hand top corner, a satiric coat-of-arms containing crossed axes, halters, and a guillotine. A picture

on sale in London in 1827, and described in Hone's *Every Day Book* of that year (I, 238) was apparently in the same direction, since the reversing of the buttons in the etching is mentioned. It had also satirical heraldic insignia in the upper corner of the picture but, to judge from the accompanying woodcut, the shield was different and contained a gibbet in place of the guillotine, no doubt because the use of that instrument in Scotland had been forgotten.

38. SKETCHES AT LORD LOVAT'S TRIAL   Fig. 21
   Ascribed to Hogarth
               British Museum (1842–8–6–398, L.B. 23)
Soft pen and indian ink with vermilion on the central figure; a group at the top on the left is in light pencil only. 7¼ × 11 in. (18.4 × 28 cm.)
Inscribed by Horace Walpole, below, 'Sketches of Lord Lovat's Trial by Hogarth'.
COLL.: Horace Walpole, Sale, 13 June 1842, Lot 1277, bought for the B.M. £6 15s.
REPROD.: Engraved 1 August 1791, by W. Birch.

In spite of Horace Walpole's authority, which, however, is not infallible, it is not possible to accept these sketches as by Hogarth. The sketcher is primarily interested in details of robes and insignia. The attitudes are neatly and prettily delineated without any of the force which one is entitled to expect from Hogarth in depicting such circumstances at that date, more especially in view of his attitude towards Lovat. The use of colour would also be quite exceptional. The

Fig. 21 (Cat. No. 38).   ASCRIBED TO HOGARTH (? J. HIGHMORE): SKETCHES AT LORD LOVAT'S TRIAL.   British Museum

drawing is much more in the manner of Highmore's sketches for the Procession of the Order of the Bath in the possession of Lady King as reproduced by C. R. Beard in the *Connoisseur*, May and July, 1934.

39. THE PROPORTIONS OF GARRICK AND QUIN, 1746

Plate 37
Royal Library (13477)

Pen with brown ink, closely following pencil. $8\frac{7}{8} \times 7\frac{1}{4}$ in. (22.6×18.5 cm.)

Four figures with a scale forming part of a letter on a folded sheet endorsed 'to T. H. to be left at the Post office at Norwich'. The letter reads, on the front page above the sketch:—

Oct 21, 1746.

'Sr

If the exact Figure of Mr. Quin, were to be reduc'd to the size of the print of Mr. Garrick it would seem to be the shortest man of the two, because Mr. Garrick is of a taller proportion. examples'.

Under the sketch, which has 'a very short proportion' 'Quin', 'Garrick' 'a very tall proportion' written under the figures from left to right, and a 'scale of feet' to the right of Quin, the letter continues:—

'Let these figures be doubled down so as to be seen but one at once, then let it be ask's which represents the Tallest man Yours W H'.

On the right-hand inner page (having the address on the verso) a note, also in Hogarth's hand, reads:—

'The Picture from whence the Print in question was taken, was Painted from Mr. Garrick big as the life, & was sold for two Hundred pounds on account of its Likeness, which was the reason it *was call'd Mr. Garrick in the Character of Richard the 3d*—and not any body else'.

REPROD.: Engraved in facsimile, 12 May 1797, for Laurie and Whittle and by T. Cook, 1 Nov. 1808, for *Genuine Works*, ii 280. (B.M. Sat. 2820 and 2821.)

COLL.: The reproduction of 1797 states that the letter was sent 'to a member of a Literary Society at Norwich who styled themselves the Argonauts' and that it had been purchased about two years before from the executors of the late Nathaniel Roe. *Genuine Works* i, p. 130, specifies the purchaser as Mr. Stevenson, of Norwich, and, ii, 280, says that the drawing was then (1810) the property of J. P. Kemble. Lot 76, 10th day, at the Kemble Sale, Evans, 26 Jan. et sqq., 1821, the drawing was acquired for George IV from Colnaghi (Archives Invoice 28336, 16 July 1821, £15 15s.). See also *Anecd.*, 1833, p. 395.

EXHIB.: R.I. (English Humourists), 1889, No. 2.

A document of capital importance; the letter written in Hogarth best autograph and the pen drawing in his cleanest manner. It is noticeable that the apparently extemporized character of the penwork is belied by the first drawing in pencil.

A burlesque figure of Quin, after a print of him in the character of Coriolanus, has been found in Plate I, fig. 19 of the *Analysis of Beauty* (*Anecd.*, 1833, p. 337).

40-63. INDUSTRY AND IDLENESS

Plates 41–63

Drawings for the series of twelve engravings published 30 Sept. 1747 (B.M. Satires, vol. III, pt. i, pp. 673-721) With the exception of Plate 8, the prints are all in the reverse direction from the drawings.

Of the drawings now at the British Museum, sixteen, **Nos. 41, 43-48, 50, 53-56, 58, 60, 62 and 63**, were acquired in 1896 from Messrs. Colnaghi, and are stated in the register to have been bought at the Horace Walpole Sale by Gye, and from him in 1846 by E. Cheney. This seems to require some amplification. The catalogue of the Walpole Sale, Robins, 13 June 1842, et sqq., specifies under Lot 1311 on the 10th day, the twelve prints in prior states and the original designs of the same, in all 24 in number (bought by Graves 104 gns.). The number 24 may be a misprint for 28, but the first edition of *Biogr. Anecd.*, 1781, p. 66, says that Dr. Lort had drawings of the two first subjects of this series, while Horace Walpole had the rest and two designs which were not used. This note was omitted from subsequent editions, and when Dr. Lort's drawings were sold at Leigh and Sotheby's, May 26, 1791, they were included *en bloc* in Lot 69 on the 7th day in two volumes of Hogarth's prints. The present 'Horace Walpole' series contains sketches for the first two plates, but even if these were Dr. Lort's two drawings, the discrepancy in numbers at the sale in 1842 would not be removed. *Anecd.*, 1833, p. 396, does not give the number of drawings in Walpole's collection but says explicitly that it contained 'the drawings for this set of plates except the Lord Mayor's Show. . . .' Of several there are rough sketches and more finished ones. There are two additional drawings to come in after Plate VIII. (1) 'A Cook's Shop'. (2) 'The good Apprentice in his warehouse'. The series was apparently bought at the Horace Walpole Sale by, or for, Standly, at whose sale in 1845 they appear as Lot 1099, 'sixteen sketches for the Idle and Industrious Apprentices' bought by Colnaghi £54 12s. According to the copy of the catalogue at the British Museum, they were bought by Anderdon, the name Gye being first entered and then cancelled. Presumably the sales by Gye to Cheney and subsequently by Cheney were private, since the set does not occur with other drawings by Hogarth (see on Nos. 87 and 88) at the Cheney Sale at Sotheby's on 29 April 1885.

Two further sheets (Nos. 40 and 42), presented to the British Museum by the N.A.C.F. in 1914, were previously in the Richard Johnson and Newton Robinson collections, and may, perhaps, have been those in Lort's collection referred to above. Four, not previously recorded, are in the collection of the Marquess of Exeter, with, conjecturally, a fifth (No. 64), a repetition of which is in the Pierpont Morgan Library in New York (No. 65).

In all, therefore, 22 sheets, with 24 drawings, for this series, and two conjecturally belonging to it, have been preserved. No drawing for Plate 12, the Lord Mayor's Procession, has been preserved or is recorded.

40. THE FELLOW 'PRENTICES AT THEIR LOOMS

Sketch for pl. 1
Plate 41
British Museum (1914-6-13-30)

Pen and brown ink and grey washes over pencil. Details separately sketched in the margins in pen and brown ink. $10\frac{3}{8} \times 13$ in. (26.3×33 cm.)

'Goodchild', 'Barnwell', with erasure 'Thomas Th . . .' in pencil in the margin under the characters.

On the reverse a very rough chalk sketch for Plate 7, see No. 52.

COLL.: Possibly Dr. Lort (see above); Richard Johnson (Platt, 23 April 1912, et sqq. Lot 638), and C. Newton

Robinson (Christie's, 6 April 1914, Lot 18. 59 guineas).
The details in which this sketch differs from the finished drawing and the print are mainly minor and in the accessories; the most important is in the face of the master who is here represented, as in the print and the story, without remarkable character, while in No. 41 he is evidently brutal. The stick in his right hand and other details show that the need for reversal was overlooked. The ornaments in the frame were not reversed in the print.

41. THE SAME   Plate 42
    Finished drawing for pl. 1
           British Museum (1896–7–10–2. L.B.1)
Pen and grey wash over pencil. Incised, the heads with special care. Perspective lines in pencil. $10\frac{7}{8} \times 14$ in. (27.6×35.6 cm.)
Ornaments in the border as in the print. Inscribed below: 'The Fellow Prentices at their Looms. Representing Industry and Idleness'. The tankard inscribed 'John . . . Crown & . . . in Spittle Fields'.
See on No. 40.

42. THE INDUSTRIOUS 'PRENTICE PERFORMING THE DUTY OF A CHRISTIAN   Plate 43
    Sketch for pl. 2   British Museum (1914–6–13–31)
Pen with brown ink and grey wash over pencil. Perspective lines in pencil, some being ruled. A vertical pencil line in the centre. $8\frac{3}{8} \times 12\frac{5}{8}$ in. (21.2×32.1 cm.) Ornaments in the margin.
COLL.: As on No. 40.

The interior is supposed to represent a view from one of the small ornamental galleries beside the choir of St. Martin's Church, a large part of the body of the church being imaginatively transported into that situation.

43. THE SAME   Plate 44
    Finished drawing for pl. 2
           British Museum (1896–7–10–4. L.B.2)
Pencil, pen and grey wash. Incised in places. A vertical line or fold in the centre. $10\frac{3}{4} \times 13\frac{3}{4}$ in. (27.3×35 cm.)
Ornaments in the border as (reversed) in the print. Inscribed below: 'The good Prentice at church performing the duty of a Christian'.

In the sketch, the church has a flat roof, that in the finished drawing and the print is vaulted. On the left, the prayer book held by the fat woman is converted into a fan, the back-view of the head and shoulders of a seated woman becomes a singing old man seen from the front, and a sleeping youth, perhaps the Idle Apprentice, is squeezed into the Good Apprentice's pew; all rather forced incidents which are further elaborated in the print. This pew is given a door, thus evading the pose of the Apprentice's legs, at once florid and clumsy in the sketch. On the right the hat, which hangs somewhat inappropriately above the old woman in the earlier drawing, disappears from the present drawing and reappears in the print on the side of the pew, while its place above the old woman is taken by an architectural circle.

44. THE IDLE 'PRENTICE AT PLAY IN THE CHURCHYARD DURING DIVINE SERVICE
                               Plate 45
    Sketch for pl. 3 British Museum (1896–7–10–6; L.B.3)
Pen with brown ink and grey wash over pencil, within ruled pencil border and squared. Apparently corrections and additions in pen with black ink. A vertical pencil ruled line and perspective lines, the ruler used for the windows. $8\frac{1}{2} \times 11\frac{5}{8}$ in. (21.6×29.5 cm.)

The pen work is noticeably free, loosely indicating form, over the pencil drawing with broken flourishes; the grouping of the players unusually intense and concentrated, with the beadle balancing the composition and illustrating the text but, perhaps inevitably, on a subordinate plane and ineffective.

45. THE SAME   Plate 46
    Finished drawing for pl. 3
           British Museum (1896–7–10–7; L.B.4)
Pen and grey wash over pencil. Closely incised and with traces of squaring. The figure at the door is detailed in pen and brown ink. $10\frac{3}{4} \times 13\frac{7}{8}$ in. (27.3×35.2 cm.)
Ornaments in the border as in Nos. 40, 42 and 43 and, reversed, in print. Inscribed below: 'The bad Prentice at play in the Churchyard with Pickpockets'.
REPROD.: A. Dobson, 1902, p. 210.

The attitudes of the two crouching villains by the tombstone have been altered, becoming more purposive, and the background group entering the church is made more orderly; otherwise the scene seems to have been presented complete from the first. The beadle holds his cane in his left hand with a view to reversal in the print.

46. THE INDUSTRIOUS 'PRENTICE A FAVOURITE AND ENTRUSTED BY HIS MASTER   Plate 47
    Sketch for pl. 4
           British Museum (1896–7–10–9; L.B.5)
Pencil, pen and brown ink and grey wash. Ruled perspective lines. $8\frac{1}{2} \times 11\frac{1}{2}$ in. (21.6×29.2 cm.).
The figure of the master inscribed, below, 'A Quaker'.

The pen-work in the principal figures is more advanced and careful than in the preceding preparatory studies, but very free in the background incidents. The grey wash, single, except in the hats, already indicates the lighting. The apprentice holds his pen in, and the master points with, the left hand, but the composition is clearly left to right in intention and the effect is injured by reversal in the print.

47. THE SAME   Plate 48
    Possibly the final drawing for pl. 4
           British Museum (1896–7–10–10; L.B.6)
Pencil, pen and grey wash, the ruler used, carefully incised with the stylus. $8\frac{1}{2} \times 11\frac{1}{2}$ in. (21.6×29.2 cm.)
REPROD.: A. Dobson, 1902, p. 212.

Though possibly the final stage before the print, this drawing is much more free and sketchy than the other finished drawings; the pen-work is more summary, and the faces, etc., are not modelled nor the features carefully outlined. At the same time, the curved flourishes of the previous drawing have disappeared.
Compared with the sketch, the legs of the porter are shown, the background has been altered and considerably detailed, the sleeping dog has been replaced by the incident of a dog and cat, the apprentice holds a key in place of a pen, and the objects on the escritoire have been changed. All these details are carried into the print where, also, the master is given a less Quakerlike costume. In fact, his personality has undergone

a change as in pl. 1. In the print, too, the almanac has been altered, and both it and the half-open book have been lettered.

48. THE IDLE 'PRENTICE TURNED AWAY AND SENT TO SEA   Plate 49
Sketch and possibly final drawing for pl. 5

British Museum (1896–7–10–12; L.B.7)

Grey wash, a little pen, over rough pencil within pencil border. Incised; $8\frac{1}{2} \times 11\frac{1}{2}$ in. (21.6 × 29.2 cm.)

A circle in pencil around the ships and rowing boat in the distance above the rower's shoulder marks the details which were to be replaced in the print by a gallows. The outstretched hand has been altered as an afterthought in the drawing to point to this. In the print, the rope's end is untwisted into tails, and the paper, already indicated in pen as an afterthought in the drawing, is lettered 'This Indenture'. These corrections suggest that this was the final drawing, rough though it might be left.

49. THE INDUSTRIOUS 'PRENTICE OUT OF HIS TIME AND MARRIED TO HIS MASTER'S DAUGHTER   Plate 51
Sketch for pl. 6

The Marquess of Exeter

Pencil and pen with black ink, no wash, on white paper. Roughly incised and reddened at the back. Lines ruled with stylus only in the front of the house, the ruler also used with pencil and pen in places. Many alterations. $8\frac{1}{4} \times 11\frac{5}{8}$ in. (21.1 × 29.6 cm.) on paper $9\frac{7}{8} \times 12\frac{5}{8}$ in. (25.2 × 32 cm.) In the ninth Earl of Exeter's MS. list (1782) of his Hogarth prints, under Original Drawings. See on No. 50.

50. THE SAME   Plate 52
Further sketch for pl. 6

British Museum (1896–7–10–14. L.B.8)

Pen and brown and grey washes over pencil; perspective lines in pencil and the ruler used freely. Incised in part. $8\frac{1}{2} \times 11\frac{1}{2}$ in. (21.6 × 29.2 cm.)

REPROD.: A. Dobson, 1902, p. 214.

The standing woman on the extreme right is here accompanied by a child with a doll and a dog instead of wheeling a barrow as in No. 49; the drummer nearest to her is reduced in size, and the flying hats above the crowd are omitted with the detailing of the architecture. The drummer receiving pay is also reduced in size, and his right hand with hat, lowered. The window is enlarged, and the bride indicated; the post in the foreground is reduced. On the left, the woman receiving alms and her children are respectively diminished in size and number.

In the print, besides the introduction of numerous details, the woman and child on the right in No. 50 and the drummer next to her are replaced by a cul-de-jatte (the dog remaining in another attitude), and by a pair of musical butchers, one of whom is quarrelling with a 'cellist who has replaced the nearest drummer. One of the hats raised above the crowd is restored from the preliminary stage, No. 49.

Except for the serving man on the extreme right, who is dispensing the broken meats with his right hand, reversal appears to have been kept in mind throughout the drawing; the bridegroom paying the drummer with his left hand, and

the drummers having their instruments over the right knee. While the general idea and disposition remain unaltered from the first, the changes on the left hand of the drawing would appear to be made in order to give adequate prominence to the central figures, but those on the right hand replace commonplace figures by more characteristic, and introduce a new incident. None the less, there are more variety and depth in the background figures of the first sketch, taken simply as a crowd, than in the later version.

51. THE IDLE 'PRENTICE RETURNED FROM SEA AND IN A GARRET WITH A COMMON PROSTITUTE   Plate 53
Sketch for pl. 7   The Marquess of Exeter

On the reverse of No. 57. Pencil $8\frac{1}{4} \times 11\frac{3}{8}$ in. (21 × 29 cm.) within rough pencil border; the sheet $9\frac{7}{8} \times 13$ in. (25 × 33 cm.) Watermark: 'Pro Patria'.

Two figures are roughly indicated on a bed, but their action is not intelligible; it is not even certain that their legs are extended, and the near figure rather than the further appears to be the man. The timbers propped against the door are already clearly discernible; but the disturbing incident would seem at this stage to be the appearance of a head and shoulders at a window in the corner.

52. THE SAME, a further stage.   Plate 54
British Museum

On the reverse of No. 40. Pencil.

While the scene remains the same, except that the ceiling has clearly become the roof of an attic, the fireplace and the cat jumping into it from the chimney, which constitute the keynote to the whole plate, have been introduced. At the same time the prentice is holding up his hands in horror and his companion is clearly contemplating her spoils. The foot of the bed is shown to be foundering, and objects are indicated in the foreground, but a rectangular arrangement at the head of the bed remains over, rather heightened, from the previous stage, and there are scrawls upon it suggesting some kind of ornament.

53. THE SAME   Plate 55
An advanced drawing for pl. 7

British Museum (1896–7–10–16. L.B.9)

Pen, brown and grey washes over pencil within a ruled pencil border. Some additions in pencil. A vertical pencil line in the centre; the ruler used freely. Incised with the stylus. $8\frac{3}{8} \times 11\frac{5}{8}$ in. (21.3 × 29.5 cm.)

The incidents are now nearly identical with those of the print. Both characters are now turned towards the spectator; a suspended sword at the head of the bed, no doubt intended in allegory, takes the places of the mysterious rectangles in the previous sketches, and was originally carried into the print where both it and the key beside it are discernible under the hoop which finally replaced it. Shortening of the bed in order to show more floor space is already indicated in the drawing by a broad brush line; and fresh bed-posts are added towards the foot, that on the near side being marked in pencil for replacement by the jug which appears in the print together with other objects.

54. THE INDUSTRIOUS 'PRENTICE GROWN RICH AND SHERIFF OF LONDON   Plate 56
Sketch for pl. 8
                    British Museum (1896–7–10–18. L.B.10)
Pen, brown and grey washes over slight red chalk and pencil. The red chalk perhaps only as an indication of perspective. The stylus used for incision with the ruler. 8½ × 11½ in. (21.6 × 29.2 cm.)
REPROD.: A. Dobson, 1902, p. 216.

Here, as in another banquet scene, that of the *Election* pictures, the original direction is preserved in the prints, while all the other prints in the two series are reversed. This might be due to an intention of retaining right and left hands for the knives and forks of the feasters. In this drawing, however, these implements are universally dispensed with as superfluous. Their introduction, and that of a black serving-boy, together with the definition of the industrious prentice as sheriff with his wife seated in the far distance, indicate that there was an intervening drawing before the engraving, but the scene is already fully realized. Here, as in No. 58, Hogarth's pictorial imagination outpaced his dramatic.

55. THE INDUSTRIOUS 'PRENTICE, WHEN A MERCHANT, GIVING MONEY TO HIS PARENTS   Plate 57
                    British Museum (1876–7–10–28. L.B.15)
A subject in the same series, but not engraved.
Pen with brown ink and grey wash over pencil. 8½ × 11½ in. (21.6 × 29.2 cm.)
REPROD.: A. Dobson, 1902, opp. p. 222.

According to *Anecd.*, 1833, p. 396, this and the next subject were intended to come after Plate 8 of the series.

56. THE IDLE 'PRENTICE STEALING FROM HIS MOTHER   Plate 58
                    British Museum (1896–7–10–29. L.B.16)
Another subject in the same series, but not engraved.
Pen with brown ink and grey wash over pencil. A vertical pencil line ruled in the centre. The sign-board over the shop-front inscribed 'Roast and Boil'd' and a receptacle held by the thief's accomplice, 'Fowler's Cook-shop' (*cf.* No. 63). 8⅜ × 11⅝ in. (21.3 × 29.5 cm.)
REPROD.: A. Dobson, 1902, opp. p. 208, 1907, opp. p. 250 (*q.v.*).
See on No. 55.

57. THE INDUSTRIOUS 'PRENTICE MARRIED AND FURNISHING HIS HOUSE   Plate 50
                    The Marquess of Exeter
A subject in the same series, not engraved.
Pen with brown ink and grey wash within rough pen border. 8¼ × 11⅜ in. (21 × 29 cm.)
For the reverse, see No. 51.
In the ninth Earl of Exeter's MS. list, 1782.

58. THE IDLE 'PRENTICE BETRAYED BY HIS WHORE AND TAKEN IN A NIGHT CELLAR WITH HIS ACCOMPLICE   Plate 59
Sketch for pl. 9
                    British Museum (1896–7–10–20. L.B.11)
Pen with brown ink and grey wash over pencil. 10⅜ × 12¾ in. (26.4 × 32.4 cm.)
See on No. 59.

59. THE SAME   Plate 60
Further sketch for pl. 9   The Marquess of Exeter
Black and white chalk, discoloured, on blue paper, within ruled border, incised, and the back blackened. A pencilled horizontal line towards the centre, the ruler used in rafter and steps. 8½ × 11⅜ in. (21.5 × 29 cm.) on a sheet 9⅝ × 12¼ in. (24.5 × 31 cm.)
In the ninth Earl of Exeter's MS. list, 1782.

The drawing loose and coarse, but very detailed in places. Clearly an advanced, if not the final stage, and much stronger than the drawing on similar paper for the *Don Quixote* series (No. 35).
In this case, the coarser drawing represents the more advanced stage and, indeed, except for the elimination of the sword which, in the drawing, would effectually prevent the transmission of the corpse into the cellar and the addition of the mace in the magistrate's hand and other small details, this drawing is virtually reproduced in the print. In the version at the British Museum (No. 58) there is nothing to suggest an arrest; it is merely a tavern scene in which the idle apprentice is represented as nefariously engaged. The much more presentable hostess is merely pouring out a drink for a conceivable tipstaff. At the same time, the general disposition of the scene remains the same.
The somewhat remarkable kneeling attitude of the idle apprentice in both these drawings recurs in the figure at the foot on the left of the *Reward of Cruelty* (No. 74).

60. THE INDUSTRIOUS 'PRENTICE ALDERMAN OF LONDON, THE IDLE ONE BROUGHT BEFORE HIM AND IMPEACHED BY HIS ACCOMPLICE   Plate 61
Sketch for pl. 10
                    British Museum (1896–7–10–22. L.B.12)
Pen with brown ink and grey wash over pencil. 8½ × 11½ in. (21.6 × 29.2 cm.).
See on No. 61.

61. THE SAME   Plate 62
Further sketch for pl. 10   The Marquess of Exeter
Pencil on white paper with 'Pro Patria' watermark, folded in every direction, within pencil border, ruler not used, fully incised and the back reddened. 9½ × 11½ in. (24.1 × 29.2 cm.) on sheet 9⅞ × 13 in. (25 × 33 cm.)
On the back of the paper 'To Mrs. Whatrell', the name indistinct.
In the ninth Earl of Exeter's MS. list, 1782.

As with the drawings for Plate 9, the loose pencil drawing represents a later stage than the pen drawing, and is almost identical in its general features with the final drawing and the print from it in reverse. The anguished mother is not yet recognizable, and neither the beadle nor the constable hold up their staff and incriminating weapons, but the main actions are already indicated. In the earlier pen drawing, on the contrary, even the idle apprentice is scarcely distinguishable in the crowd beyond the barrier, while the bribe-accepting attendant has much less character. Yet the general design remains the same throughout, and the furniture and architecture are retained in the pencil stage and to some extent even persist throughout into the print, where they accord exceedingly badly with the revision of the incidents. The clerk in the print cannot sit at the table, and the columns, etc., have become an open colonnade. It is noticeable that the fire buckets persist throughout.

The clerk's left hand used for writing and the false witness's right on the Bible, show that reversal was intended.

62. THE SAME   Plate 63
Finished drawing for pl. 10
British Museum (1896–7–10–23. L.B.13)

Pen with brown ink, with brown and grey washes. Carefully incised, the ruler used freely. $8\frac{1}{2} \times 11\frac{1}{2}$ in. (21.6×29.2 cm.)
REPROD.: A. Dobson, 1902, opp. p. 218.
See on No. 61.

63. THE IDLE 'PRENTICE EXECUTED AT TYBURN
Plate 64
Finished drawing for pl. 11
British Museum (1896–7–10–25. L.B.14)

Pen and grey wash, emphasized in places in black ink; incised with the stylus. Some green paint splashes. $9\frac{1}{8} \times 15\frac{3}{8}$ in. (23.2×39 cm.)

'The last dying speech and confession of Thomas Fowler' inscribed on the paper held by a woman in the foreground.
A figure in the cart with Idle, where the print has a Wesleyan preacher exhorting him, has been erased; the wall and on-lookers, which appear in the print on the left above the horse-man, are lightly indicated, as an afterthought, in pencil, and there are also minor modifications in the print. The drawing is wooden throughout and inferior to the print, but there is no need to suspect that it is a reversed copy from the print, however much it and similar 'final stages' may owe to assistants.

64. AN OPERATION SCENE IN A HOSPITAL Plate 65
The Marquess of Exeter

Pencil, shaded. Some portions enforced with blacker pencil; within ruled border. Incised and reddened behind. A court-yard with colonnades within another border at foot, right. $8\frac{5}{8} \times 11\frac{3}{8}$ in. (21.9×29 cm.) on a sheet with 'G.R. Pro Patria' watermark, measuring approximately $11\frac{3}{4} \times 16$ in. (29.8×41 cm.)
Inscribed in pen by the ninth Earl of Exeter 'Sketch for the *Harlot's Progress* but never engraved'. Not in his MS. list.

The drawing was clearly intended for an engraving, for the surgeon is using his left hand in cauterizing, and the doctor's sword, which may be indicated in this drawing, is clearly on his right hip in the finished version, No. 65. This alone is sufficient to dissociate these two drawings from the *Harlot's Progress*, for that series was engraved from the oil paintings which are now destroyed. Moreover, the size is considerably smaller than that of the *Harlot's Progress*, and is the same as that of the *Industry and Idleness* drawings, and the courtyard in the small inset, which can have no connection with a hos-pital ward, seems to recall or foreshadow the setting of the unused design in that series, the Apprentice giving money to his parents, No. 55. The free and capable draughtsmanship also belongs to the later date.
There is nothing to show whether the patient is a man or a woman. The joke of setting fire to the doctor's wig, which is said to have actually occurred on Queen Caroline's deathbed, is used in *Tristram Shandy*, c. xlvi, and was too good to miss, whatever the context.

65. THE SAME, the central figures altered   Plate 66
Pierpont Morgan Library III, 35

Pencil and grey wash over red chalk indications, within ruled pencil border, on paper with the Vryheyt mark of the firm of B. Cramer, with the countermark of the British royal cypher (Churchill, *Watermarks*, p. 47). $8\frac{5}{8} \times 11\frac{3}{4}$ in. (21.9×29.8 cm.)
Inscribed on the reverse by Fairfax Murray with the attribu-tion to Hogarth and a statement that the drawing was pur-chased at the Forman sale.
Probably Horace Walpole Collection (Sale 1842, Lot 1329, 'an original sketch by Hogarth of a Surgeon operating on an ulcered leg of a woman' (with No. 67) bought Graves £6 6s.). See also *Anecd.*, 1833, p. 393; and Standly (Sale 1845, Lot 1307), 'The Operation, a sketch in indian ink', bought Col. G [*sic*] £1 1s. Forman, see above.
REPROD.: Pierpont Morgan Library *Cat.*, III, 35. Tietze, *European Master Drawings in the United States* (1947), Plate 109.

The two central figures, the doctor and the intoxicated or overtired attendant setting his wig on fire, which were already altered in the previous drawing from which this may have been traced, have been redrafted in order to bring out the incident more clearly. The attendant's candle is raised higher in order to reach the doctor's head, his whole attitude has been altered and the small table removed. The remainder of the drawing is unchanged, except that the hands of the sur-geon have been made clearer and their position slightly shifted. It cannot be said that the changes are an improve-ment; the doctor's attitude becoming more purely rhetorical and his action inappropriate and conventional, while the spatial relations between the three figures are less well defined. At the same time, the pattern of the figures has been improved and, so far as can be judged from the photograph, the pencil work is at once lighter, more economical and more expressive, and the wash more decorative, than in any other known drawing by Hogarth. If it were not that the attendant's arm were already as perfectly delineated in the previous sketch, it might have been suspected that, in this case, the further stage, the preparation for an intended engraving, has been entrusted to one of his skilled French assistants. French influence is also suggested in the figure of the male attendant. However that may be, the technical methods are very different from the rigid outline and heavily marked features of faces in other drawings which served as final stages for Hogarth's prints.

66. ARMS FOR THE FOUNDLING HOSPITAL, 1747
Plate 38
The Marquess of Exeter

Sketch for the engraved arms of the hospital. *Cf.* Nichols and Wray, *History of the Foundling Hospital*, p. 251.
Pen on paper of irregular shape and much folded. Approxi-mately $6\frac{1}{4} \times 7$ in. (16×17.7 cm.)
Inscribed after an erasure 'Armes for (over 'of') the Found-ling Hospital; Wm. Hogarth Invt 1747'. The motto 'Help' on the scroll beneath the arms and 'Nature', 'a Lamb', 'Britannia' above the figures are also in Hogarth's writing. Below the drawing in the book where it still remains Lord Exeter has written: 'Original drawing given to Lord Exeter by Mrs. Hogarth in 1781'.
Engraved in facsimile by Richard Livesay, 1781, as from the

original in the collection of the Earl of Exeter. See also *Genuine Works*, III, 138, with a reprint, *Biogr. Anecd.*, 1782, p. 323, and *Anecd.*, 1833, p. 225 and 396.

For the figure of Nature see No. 22.

A copy at the Foundling Hospital 'presented by E. Bellamy' which possesses the erasure before 'Armes' but not the cancelled 'of' has, written below, 'These armes are to be altered by the Desire of the Committee—a Wolf in Fleecy Hosiery (erasure) is to be substituted for the Lamb and the Supporters are to [be] taken away'. A facsimile print with this inscription is in the Royal Library.

A drawing, in Indian ink, of the Foundlings ($4\frac{1}{4} \times 8\frac{1}{4}$ in.), the head-piece to a power-of-attorney for the Hospital, engraved by F. M. La Cave after Hogarth, was given to the Red Cross Sale, 19 April 1915, by Judge and Mrs. Evans (Lot 784, bought Pollard £5 5s.), perhaps the drawing in the Standly collection (Sale 1845, Lot 988, bought Graves £5 5s.) and Capel Cure Sale 1905, Lot 103 with another, bought Tregaskis, £2 10s. Stated in *Anecd.*, 1833 (p. 395), to have been in the possession of Robert Wilkinson, for whom it was engraved by J. Stow in 1826.

67. HEADPIECE TO THE *JACOBITE'S JOURNAL*, 1747   Plate 40

Royal Library (13457)

Drawing for the woodcut at the head of Fielding's weekly newspaper 'The Jacobite's Journal', the first number of which appeared on 5 December 1747. (B.M. Sat. Vol. III, Pt. I, No. 2893).

Red chalk, the paper impressed with a plate-mark, folded and torn. $8\frac{1}{4} \times 6\frac{3}{4}$ in. (21×17 cm.)

COLL.: Horace Walpole, Sale 1842, Lot 1329, with another (No. 65), bought Graves £6 6s. Standly, Sale 1845, Lot 1093, bought Colnaghi with the woodcut £1.

LIT.: *Anecd.* 1833, p. 396.

EXHIB.: Spring Gardens (Humour Exh.) 1925, No. 2. Edinburgh (King's Pictures) 1947, No. 109.

A rough border encloses the figures, which are drawn separately in two rows, in such a way as possibly to indicate that the lower group is to be brought up and placed in front of the higher. This is made clearer by the repetition of the ass's head. The sketch, which is in Hogarth's strongest extempore manner, must have required considerable elucidation even for the production of the coarse woodcut, in which the figure of the man on the ass is much altered and the object that he is waving made clear as a cap, the woman is made to hold her sword erect, and her banner is inscribed 'Harrington' and adorned with a rowel and fleurs-de-lys. In the print too the object suspended from the halter is inscribed 'London Evening Post' and is brought nearer the open jaws of the ass whose legs are differently arranged; also an elaborate vista of London replaces the faint indications of landscape.

68. ST. PAUL   Fig. 22

The Marquess of Exeter

Presumed sketch for the figure of St. Paul in the picture *Paul Before Felix* at Lincoln's Inn.

Red chalk, on thick white paper. $15\frac{3}{4} \times 7\frac{1}{2}$ in. (40×19.2 cm.)

Not in the ninth Earl of Exeter's manuscript list, 1782.

The attitude and costume are very different from those in the painting, but the general idea is sufficiently similar to enable

the drawing to be accepted as an attempt by Hogarth in the unfamiliar manner of the Old Masters. The drawing is too weak and the drapery too little understood to justify any suggestion that this is a work by some earlier artist which Hogarth had found and employed for his purpose, or which had been wrongly ascribed to Hogarth through the similarity with his picture. He himself may well have converted the costume into a large, all-enveloping toga in order to hide the weakness of the drawing. In the end, however, the figure in the picture became even more clumsy. There and here an essentially rhetorical conception is expressed without eloquence of diction, even with poverty of vocabulary.

Fig. 22 (Cat. No. 68).   HOGARTH: ST. PAUL.
The Marquess of Exeter

69. PAUL BEFORE FELIX (1748–52)   Fig. 23
                     Pierpont Morgan Library III, 38

Drawing connected with the painting in Lincoln's Inn Hall of 1748, and the engravings by Hogarth and Luke Sullivan (both of 5 February 1752), that by Hogarth in reverse.
Red chalk. 15⅜×20⅛ in. (39×51.1 cm. approximately equal to the prints).

COLL.: Joly, Fairfax Murray (*cf*. A. Dobson, 1907, p. 254). *Biogr. Anecd.* first edition, 1781 (p. 66) mentions as in Dr. Lort's Collection a drawing of *Paul Before Felix*, 'with variations from both the prints, an assessor being inserted in the space originally occupied by Drusilla', and another at one time in the possession of Mr. Dupont, a merchant, 'which he purchased for 20 guineas and bound up with a set of Hogarth's prints subsequently sold at Baker's (in 1760) for £17'. These may be the same. Lort's Collection was sold in 1791 (see on No. 71). Drawings in red chalk of both the *Paul Before Felix* and its companion, *Pharaoh's Daughter*, formed Lots 48 and 49 on the fifth day in Dr. Monro's sale, 30 April 1792, and five following days at Greenwood's, where they were said to have been given to Dr. Monro by Hogarth.

These may have been the two red chalk drawings Lots 99 and 100 at the Capel Cure sale 1905, bought for £9 5s. and £11 by Harvey.

None of the commentators account for the differences between the picture in Lincoln's Inn Hall and the two prints of the same day, except with regard to the absence from Luke Sullivan's plate of the figure of Drusilla which occurs both in the picture and in Hogarth's own plate. This drawing is alone in having a figure of a second assessor in place of Drusilla; but in all other respects it agrees with Hogarth's plate which is in reverse, even in the very important details such as the scribes and the accuser and his lectern in which Hogarth, unlike Sullivan, departs from the picture. Presumably different drawings were prepared, whether by Hogarth himself or another, from the picture, for the purposes of engraving, and this may be one of them.

In the drawing Felix is dropping, in astonishment, the paper from his right hand—a refinement which does not occur in either of the prints, and suggests a later stage. In the drawing the scroll which hangs over the scribes' desk has a full inscription. There is none in Hogarth's print (the detail does not occur in the picture nor in Sullivan's print).

Fig. 23 (Cat. No. 69).   ASCRIBED TO HOGARTH: PAUL BEFORE FELIX.   Pierpont Morgan Library

70. THE FIRST STAGE OF CRUELTY   Plate 67
The Marquess of Exeter

Drawing for the engraving, after Hogarth, of 1 February 1751 (B.M. Sat. 3147) in reverse; Plate 1 of the *Four Stages of Cruelty.*

Pencil over rough red chalk on white paper with GR and Pro Patria watermark. Incised, and the back reddened; the stylus used with the ruler alone in the architecture. $14\frac{3}{8} \times 11\frac{3}{4}$ in. (36.5×30 cm.) on a sheet $15\frac{3}{4} \times 11\frac{3}{4}$ in. (40×30 cm.)

In the ninth Earl of Exeter's manuscript list, 1782.

In all the main features the drawing is followed by the print. The chief differences are that there is only one figure on the balustrade to the left of the lamp-post, and this appears to be a woman with a basket on her head, where in the print there are two boys torturing a bird; a signpost with board where the print has a bunch of grapes, and in general the structure of the balustrade. The cat-throwing incident on the roof may have been indicated but obliterated by injury. The faces of the principal figures, including that of the boy offering a tart, who has been identified by commentators as the Prince of Wales (George III), are already made out. The pencil work is sensitive and rounded, and the action fairly forcible though there is no connection between the groups, and the spatial relations are obscure. Where the action is violent, as in the struggling dog, and the dog worrying the cat, the pencil is blacker and has become an expressive but almost indistinguishable maze of lines.

71. THE SAME   Plate 68
Pierpont Morgan Library III, 32 (*b*)

Red chalk. $14 \times 11\frac{7}{8}$ in. (35.6×30.2 cm.)

COLL.: Joly, Fairfax Murray. Two drawings for the *Cruelty* series were exhibited by Fairfax Murray at Whitechapel in 1906.

According to *Biogr. Anecd.* 1781, p. 66 (omitted in later editions), drawings for the *Four Stages of Cruelty*, together with other subjects which correspond with *Paul Before Felix, Beer Street* and *Gin Lane*, all in the Pierpont Morgan Collection (Nos. 69, 76 and 77), were in the collection of Dr. Lort. Individual drawings are not specified in his volumes of Hogarth's works sold by Leigh and Sotheby, 26 May 1791, and six following days, Lot 69 on the seventh day.

REPROD.: *Pierpont Morgan Portfolio,* 44. *Master-Drawings,* etc. Albright Art Gallery, 1935, No. 67.

The drawing is closely reproduced in the print, even the features of the boys being identical; but, in the print, there are boys torturing a bird on the balustrade, the principal instrument of torture has become an arrow, a bow is placed against the balustrade, *Nero* is added after *Tom* on the wall, and a badge with 'S.G.' is placed on the shoulder of the boy in the centre. The head of the man clapping on the cock, which appears both in the earlier drawing (No. 70) and the print, is absent from the present drawing, but there would appear to be indications that the drawing has suffered at this spot.

Fairfax Murray in the preface to the Catalogue of the Pierpont Morgan drawings implies that some, if not all, of the drawings by Hogarth in his collection which came from Dr. Joly of Dublin may have previously belonged to Hogarth's friend, Lord Charlemont. In the catalogue of Dr. Joly's Sale, at Sotheby's, 18 and 19 February 1892, Lot 142 contained twenty-five volumes of Hogarth's works. Two of these are explicitly described as consisting of Lord Charlemont's Collection, which included ten drawings. Another contained 126 drawings, and there were further drawings scattered through the remaining volumes. Among the 126 drawings the original designs of *Paul Before Felix, Progress of Cruelty, Beer Street* and *Gin Lane*, possibly Dr. Lort's (see above) were specified. Of Fairfax Murray's other drawings from the Joly Collection, three, namely *Cumbers* (No. 36), *The Husband's Return* (by Highmore, a companion to his *Enraged Husband* at the British Museum), and the *Painter Bleeding* (not by Hogarth, perhaps by Mercier), could not have been among Lord Charlemont's, since they came respectively from the Esdaile, Catterson Smith and Standly Collections. It would therefore be a fair inference that the remaining drawings described by Murray as from the Joly Collection, came equally from among the 126 and not from the two Charlemont volumes.

72. THE SECOND STAGE OF CRUELTY   Plate 69
Pierpont Morgan Library III, 32(*c*)

Drawing for the engraving in reverse after Hogarth of 1 February 1751, pl. 2 of the *Four Stages of Cruelty* (B.M. Sat. 3153).

Red chalk, incised, the back heavily reddened with chalk, watermark, fleur-de-lys and IV. The sign inscribed 'Thavies Inn'. $14 \times 11\frac{7}{8}$ in. (35.6×30.2 cm.)

COLL.: As No. 71.

Even more closely followed by the print than the preceding, the differences being such as could have been made on the plate. A pipe, pilaster and placards with inscriptions are placed on the nearest house, the man riding pillion on the ass carries a trunk on his head, while another man prods the animal with a pitchfork, and the number of the sedan chair is changed in both places to 24 and 'G.R.' and 'Tom Nero' are added. In the print the drawing of the distant figures is noticeably more careful.

73. THE THIRD STAGE OF CRUELTY   Plate 70
Pierpont Morgan Library III, 32 (*d*)

Drawing for the engraving, in reverse, after Hogarth, of 1 February 1751, pl. 3 of the *Four Stages of Cruelty* (B.M. Sat. 3159).

Red chalk, incised and squared. $14\frac{1}{8} \times 11\frac{7}{8}$ in. (35.9×30.2 cm.)

COLL.: As No. 71.

This is clearly the drawing for the engraving on copper, and not for the woodcut dated a month earlier. There is no yew tree in the woodcut as here and in the engraving, and it shows considerably less at the foot and on one side. In the woodcut the clock has two figures of the date, and the motto, which is different from that in the drawing, is below its face; in the engraving there is neither date nor motto, though there is a space above for the latter, and the hour numerals IV and IX which are absent from the drawing are supplied. In the engraving the head of the last man under the clock, which is invisible in the drawing, is clearly defined, the profile hidden in the drawing by Nero's collar is completed, and the man who is showing the knife wears a cap and no wig. The two former differences, together with the initials 'E.G.' for 'A.G.' (Ann Gill) on the travelling case at the foot of the drawing suggest an assistant's hand; but it is not possible to judge adequately from a photograph.

74. THE REWARD OF CRUELTY   Plate 71

Royal Library (13494)

Drawing for the woodcut (B.M. Sat. 3166 and 3167), in reverse, by J. Bell after Hogarth, 1 January 1750 (1751), intended as the fourth plate of the series 'Stages of Cruelty', subsequently published 1 February 1751 in the form of engravings.

The upper part mainly in pen with brown ink and some grey wash; the lower in brush, with grey; pencil indications mainly visible in the upper part, some being ruled and some apparently for alterations. Loosely incised with the stylus and stained red, especially where torn or cut through with the stylus showing that the paper had been reddened at the back. $18\frac{1}{8} \times 15\frac{1}{8}$ in. (46.3×38.3 cm.)

COLL.: S. Ireland, Sale 1797, Lot 127; 'a very fine original drawing made for one of the (*Cruelty*) woodcuts', according to *Genuine Works* III, 205, sold for £8 18s. 6d. and *Last Stage of Cruelty by Hogarth, Fine*, Lot 302 on the fourth day of the second Ireland Sale 1801, sold for £3 3s. In the Royal Collection by 1833 (*Anecd.* 1833, p. 397).

The drawing was clearly made for the woodcut, as is shown by the dimensions and by certain small details in which the engraving departs from the woodcut—e.g. the hook of the pulley which is transposed with the ring in the engraving, and the contents of the pail in which the woodcut's alterations from the drawing, perhaps a 'pentimento', have been differently treated.

The lower part of the woodcut follows on the whole closely on the drawing, with modifications as in the tablecloth, and in the two operators who have been given aprons over their clothes, and one of them spectacles. On the other hand, the upper part has been very considerably re-handled. Some of the figures remain the same, especially those at the sides, and seated at the table, but the latter have been given mortar-boards and birettas, presumably to mark their indifference to death. Those in the centre and the skeleton in the niche above them have been entirely replaced by the President on his throne and the royal arms above it, thereby altering the whole effect of the plate. Pencil indications on the right hand of the drawing suggest that it was first contemplated that the throne might be inserted here.

The hatching brushwork may have been intended as a guide to the wood cutter, but it has not been consistently employed, and in some places becomes merely a wash. Left hands are used throughout for the right, and the buttons placed on the left-hand side of the coats.

75. THE SAME   Plate 72

Pierpont Morgan Library III, 32(*e*)

Drawing for the engraving, in reverse, after Hogarth, of 1 February 1751, pl. 4 of the *Four Stages of Cruelty* (B.M. Sat. 3166).

Red chalk, incised and squared. $14 \times 11\frac{7}{8}$ in. (35.6×30.2 cm.)

COLL.: As No. 71.

Precisely followed by the copper-plate and showing the same divergences from the woodcut which is proved by the drawing for it (No. 74) to be the earlier. Several details, such as the coat of arms, are more carefully delineated in the print as was noted on No. 72, and names are supplied above the skeletons in the niches. Reversal is provided for, even in the coat-of-arms.

76. BEER STREET   Plate 73

Pierpont Morgan Library III, 37

Drawing for the engraving after Hogarth of 1 February 1751 (B.M. Sat. 3126) in reverse.

Red chalk, with additions in pencil and pen. $14\frac{5}{8} \times 12$ in. (37.1×30.5 cm.)

COLL.: Joly, Fairfax Murray.

According to *Biogr. Anecd.* 1781, p. 67*, drawings of *Beer Street* and *Gin Lane* 'with considerable variations from the prints on the same subjects' were in Dr. Lort's Collection (see on No. 71). A tracing from Dr. Lort's drawing of this subject is in Lord Exeter's Collection.

The whole of the right-hand portion of the drawing and the bottom left-hand corner were completely revised in the print; no doubt the alteration was introduced into the drawing by means of a superimposed piece of paper, since the hand of the suspended Frenchman has been left over on the drawing just as was Britannia's spear in the *Hudibras Frontispiece* (No. 5). It is in red chalk, the sedan-chair and the three figures nearest to it in pencil, as is the inscription immediately below the sign of the 'Barley Mow'. 'Farthing Post' is in ink. The paper must have been of a very irregular shape. The Frenchman, etc., disappear from the second and final states of the plate; they are explicitly stated to be in the original drawing in *Biogr. Anecd.* 1781, p. 115, and later editions.

77. GIN LANE   Plate 74

Pierpont Morgan Library III, 36

Drawing for the engraving, after Hogarth, of 1 February 1751 (B.M. Sat. 3136) in reverse.

Red chalk with pencil additions. $16\frac{1}{2} \times 12$ in. (41.9×30.5 cm.)

COLL.: See Nos. 71 and 76.

In general the engraving follows the drawing closely, including the various inscriptions and legends. In the centre, however, below the undertaker's sign, the ruined wall has been brought forward, hiding the greater part of the procession, and a madman impaling a boy with a woman expostulating have been placed in front of it, behind the man with the wheelbarrow; while the last house in the row is represented as tumbling forward; a crying child is also placed in front of the coffin, and ornaments at the base of the spire. On the extreme right of the print a woman is introduced giving gin to her baby, and there are two Charity girls behind her drinking from glasses, and other figures in front of the barrels under *Kilman's* shed. In the drawing there are two male figures only at this point. An unique trial proof in the Royal Collection, apparently that mentioned by *Anecd.* 1833, p. 233, as in Baker's Sale, shows the whole of this portion left blank, indicating the stage at which this and some other alterations were made.

78. FAT MAN UPSET LIKE A TURTLE   Plate 39

The Marquess of Exeter

Pencil on white paper. $6 \times 9\frac{7}{8}$ in. (15.3×25.1 cm.)

REPROD: facsimile by Richard Livesay, 1788, reissued *Genuine Works*, iii, p. 159. *Anecd.* 1833, p. 274.

Richard Livesay, in his covering note of 1788, says that his print 'was done from a drawing which I believe is lost', and this was copied by the later commentators. The drawing is not mentioned in the Ninth Earl of Exeter's MS. list of 1782, and it has now been removed from the book of engravings and is separately mounted, without any inscription or note by Lord Exeter.

It is noticeable that Livesay's soft-ground etching is in the reverse direction from the drawing, which is contrary to his general custom, and it is therefore possible that Lord Exeter's drawing, which has the buttons on the wrong side and has marks of soft pencil work or off-set below the strong pencil, is itself over an off-set, the original of which was copied by Livesay and was subsequently lost. Against this, the fat man's left hand in the drawing and his hat are absent from the print which is, so far as an etching can be compared with a drawing, weaker throughout. Hogarth, moreover, may have himself worked over an off-set in order to have the buttons in the correct position when reversed in a print and to have the figure generally in the position required. The drawing, therefore, may be accepted as the original drawing by Hogarth, and it is of considerable interest as probably a study from memory for a figure in a print or picture of a contemporary subject—for which, however, it appears never to have been used.

79. GEORGE TAYLOR'S EPITAPH

The Marquess of Exeter
Plate 75

(*a*) *Death Giving George Taylor a Cross Buttock.*
Pen over black chalk, a red chalk scrawl on the left; a pencil shield top right. 9 × 12⅜ in. (23 × 31.5 cm.)

Plate 76

(*b*) *George Taylor Breaking the Ribs of Death.*
Pen with brown and black ink over some pencil and red chalk in places. 8⅞ × 12⅜ in. (22.5 × 31.5 cm.)
COLL.: Morrison [*sic*] (*Biogr. Anecd.* 1782, p. 326; 1785, p. 412). Not in Lord Exeter's list of 1782.
REPROD: by Richard Livesay, March 1782 with a facsimile of the manuscript epitaph, reading:

'To the Memory of/George Taylor/whose/Skill and Courage/in the/Manual-Combat/would have done Honour/ to the/Roman Circus/Incorruptable [*sic*] and Unconquerable/Learn/Heros of a higher Class/from his Example/to render/British Bravery/Invincible/

Vain all the Honours of my brow,
Victorious Wreaths farewell.
One Trip from Death has laid me low,
By whom such Numbers fell.

Still bravely I'll dispute the Prize,
Nor yield—tho' out of breath,
'Tis but a fall, I yet shall rise,
And vanquish even—Death.'

His covering note, 1788, says 'the original drawings of these prints were in the possession of a lady, who, actuated by the same generous spirit that influenced Mr. Forrest, respecting the drawings of Read and Hunt (see Nos. 30 and 88); as soon as she found they were of value, presented them to Mrs. Hogarth, who sold them to Mr. Morison [*sic*]. He, by finding them in the lady's possession, engaged the preference, and soon after sold them to the Earl of Exeter, in whose possession they now remain'. He adds that the Rev. Dr. Lort has drawings in red chalk of the same subject. Perhaps these were the transfers with Hogarth's writing mentioned by A. Dobson (1907, p. 268) as in the Fairfax Murray collection.

George Taylor, a noted boxer, died on 21 February 1750.

The epitaph, according to *Biogr. Anecd.* 1785, p. 413, was placed on his tombstone in Deptford churchyard. The breeches in the first plate and loin cloth in the second emphasize the idea in the verses. (See also *Genuine Works*, ii, 270.)

80. VIGNETTE FOR THE *ANALYSIS OF BEAUTY*, 1753

Fig. 24
Royal Library (13456)

Drawing for the engraving, in reverse, on the title-page of Hogarth's *Analysis of Beauty*, 1753.
Red chalk; some lines incised with the stylus and ruler. 6⅛ × 5½ in. (15.7 × 13.9 cm.)
The mount is inscribed in pen at foot in S. Ireland's hand, 'Frontispiece to ye Analysis—given to me by Mrs. Hogarth. Saml. Ireland'. The words inscribed under the drawing on the paper itself, also in Samuel Ireland's hand, 'Sketch of a New coinage by Hogarth 1762', cannot refer to this drawing and are hard to explain, unless they refer to a 'Sketch of his present Majesty, taken hastily on seeing the new coinage of 1764' included among Samuel Ireland's drawings by Hogarth on page 67* of the *Biogr. Anecd.* 1781, etc. There was no new coinage in 1762, nor in 1764. There was a guinea of 1761 and a very small issue of shillings in 1763.
In the Royal Collection by 1833 (*Anecd.* 1833, p. 397). Apparently not in the Ireland sales.

While the pyramid has the same dimensions as on the title-page, it is shaded and has a ring at the apex, neither of which features is carried into the engraving. The serpentine line is differently placed in the print, is given a snake-head and is no longer suspended as in the drawing by a ribbon with a somewhat extravagant bow. In the print also it is placed upon a partly shaded plinth inscribed VARIETY.

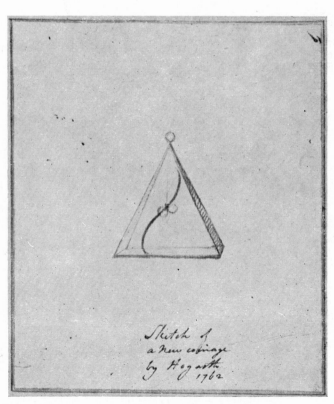

Fig. 24 (Cat. No. 80). HOGARTH: VIGNETTE FOR THE ANALYSIS OF BEAUTY. Royal Library

81. *THE ANALYSIS OF BEAUTY*

British Museum

The manuscripts of the *Analysis of Beauty* now at the British Museum (Egerton 3011-6, from the J. Ireland, G. Baker and Standly collections) consist of two holograph drafts and a fair copy, each in two volumes. The drawings are in the second draft, and are on the blank verso of the manuscript pages opposite to the text, either drawn directly on the blank leaves or on small slips of paper pasted in. In a few cases the drawings are on pages which have no manuscript on the other side. The drawings are frequently accompanied by slips containing their numbers and all the figures are numbered either in red chalk or pen; where both occur the pen numbers appear to be the earlier because cancelled by the red, and they sometimes correspond with those in the text on the opposite page. Neither the pen nor the chalk numbers correspond with those on the two engraved plates in the *Analysis* (B.M. Sat., III, Pt. 2, Nos. 3217 and 3226). Most of the subjects, however, occur in the *Analysis*, generally in reverse. Further drawings of similar type (one, 'The Vase', reproduced by J. Ireland, *Hogarth Illustrated*, iii, p. 147), are among the miscellaneous papers also at the British Museum (Add. MSS. 27992).

The following selection of drawings from the *Analysis* is made on the ground of general interest.

Fig. 25 (Cat. No. 81c).   HOGARTH: A SHEET OF FIGURES.   British Museum

VOLUME 1

(*a*) HENRY VIII, HERCULES AND A FRENCH DANCING-MASTER (Fol. 9, verso)   Plate 82

Red chalk, whole page, no writing on the recto, inscribed with erasures, 'Fig. 2', 'Fig. 1', '3' and '4' respectively, all in red. 7⅞×6¼ in. (20×16 cm.)

The figure of Henry VIII is engraved as No. 72, Plate 2 of the *Analysis*. The Hercules seen from behind is pl. 1, No. 3; the dancing-master called 'Essex' is pl. 1, No. 7. The diagram finally engraved as pl. 1, No. 47 was once intended for the space occupied by the caricature after Ghezzi (B.M. Sat., III, Pt. 2, p. 876). It is anticipated in the margin of Fol. 41 (verso) of the first draft (Egerton 3011) and repeated on Fol. 29 (verso) of the present volume.

Reproduced in facsimile, *Hogarth Illustrated*, Vol. III, p. 158.

(*b*) LAOCOON. AN ORNAMENTAL PINEAPPLE (Fol. 11, verso)   Plate 83

Red chalk, whole page, numbered '5' and '6', both in red. The Laocoon is engraved in reverse, pl. 1, No. 9; the pineapple, pl. 1, No. 10. It is repeated as a pen inset on Fol. 23 (verso).

(*c*) A SHEET OF FIGURES (Fol. 14, verso)   Fig. 25

Red chalk and pencil, whole page, numbered from left to right '10' to '16' in red, the last figure numbered '12' in red and '17' in pencil.

First thoughts: the figures numbered '10', '11', '13' and '17' are repeated in (*d*) and (*e*) below. The figure at the top

numbered '12' has been cancelled in pencil and repeated below with the same number and with the number '17', which, like the figure itself, is in pencil. It is engraved in reverse as pl. 1, No. 18. The figure on the right in the second row, originally numbered 15, has been entirely cancelled in pencil; it does not seem to occur on either of the plates. Nos. '14' and '16' are engraved as Nos. 21 and 22 on pl. 1.

(*d*) A JUDGE WRITING (Fol. 40, verso)   Fig. 26

Pen, on a page with sentences marked for insertion on Fol. 41 recto. 'Fig. 9' in pen, erased, also with the pen; numbered '1' in red.

An elaboration of the figure numbered '10' in (*c*) above; engraved in the same direction, Plate 1, No. 16.

The hesitating, trembling line is very noticeable, and seems to be intended to represent the materials of the wig, ermine, etc.

(*e*) THE 'OLD BABY', THE CHILD IN A MAN'S WIG, AND THE BALLET DANCER (Fol. 41, verso)
          Plate 77

Pen over pencil, on a page containing manuscript for insertion on Fol. 42, recto. Inscribed 'Fig. 10', 'Fig. 11' and 'Fig. 13' in pen over erasures.

Engraved as pl. 1, Nos. 17, 18 and 20. The old man as a baby crying for its spilt pap is an elaboration of the figure numbered 11 on (*c*) above. It had already been used, with some differences, in the background of the print *The Stage Coach* of 1747 (B.M. Sat., III, 1, p. 668, No. 2882), where it is carried in procession with (in one state only) the legend

Fig. 26 (Cat. No. 81d).   HOGARTH: A JUDGE WRITING.
British Museum

Fig. 27 (Cat. No. 81f).   HOGARTH: A ROMAN GENERAL
IN A PERRUQUE.   British Museum

'No Old Baby'. This is a reference to the election as member for the County of Essex of the Hon. John Child Tylney, afterwards Viscount Castlemaine, when he was only 20 years of age. (See also *infra*, No. 82.) The 'child with a man's wig and cap on' may be a repetition of those numbered 12 and 17 on (*c*) above; it is considerably altered in the engraving.

The ballet dancer was lightly sketched as '13' on (*c*) above. It recalls the engravings *Taste in High Life* and *The Charmers of the Age*, both of 1742 (B.M. Sat., III, Pt. 1, pp. 448 and 450, Nos. 2563 and 2569), where it is connected traditionally with Desnoyers the dancer. Reproduced *Hogarth Illustrated*, Vol. III, p. 162, with other figures (B.M. Sat., No. 3251).

(*f*) A ROMAN GENERAL IN A PERRUQUE (Fol. 42, verso)   Fig. 27

Pen over pencil on a page of the manuscript, inscribed 'Fig. 13, Print 1'. The '3' in red over '2' in pen.

Engraved as pl. 1, No. 19, in the same direction but the arms altered and the sword transferred to the left side; traditionally regarded as Quin in the character of Brutus.

(*g*) A CAPITAL OF HATS AND PERIWIGS (Fol. 64)   Plate 84

Pen and grey wash. Numbered '37' in red, no manuscript on verso.

Engraved in reverse as pl. 1, No. 48. A preliminary sketch in pencil is on Add. MSS. 27992, Fol. 16, verso. The idea is anticipated, as is pointed out in *Biogr. Anecd.* 1785, p. 151, in the altar on the large *Masquerade Ticket* of 1727, and is elaborated in the engraving *The Five Orders of Periwigs*, of 1751 (B.M. Sat., IV, Pt. 2, No. 3812). See also No. 94.

(*h*) SANCHO PANZA (Fol. 98, verso)   Plate 78

Red chalk, one of several figures on the page. Numbered '65' in red.

Engraved as pl. 2, No. 75, in the same direction. The figure is described by Hogarth himself (*Analysis*, p. 137) as from a French print of Sancho. As Dr. Antal has noted (*Art Bulletin, l.c.*, p. 40, n. 15) it is taken from pl. xv of Coypel's *Don Quixote* series. It had already been used by Hogarth in his print of 1742, *The Mystery of Masonry* (B.M. Sat., III, Pt. 1, p. 434, No. 2549), together with so many other figures from the same source as to justify Horace Walpole in describing the print as 'stolen from Coypel's *Don Quixote*'.

VOLUME 2

(*i*) FROM AN ANTIQUE HEAD (Fol. 28, verso)   Plate 80

Pencil, numbered in pen '85'.

Engraved as No. 97 on pl. 1 in reverse. (See on (*j*) *infra*.)

(*j*) AN OLD MAN'S HEAD BY FIAMMINGO (Fol. 29)   Plate 81

Pencil, numbered in pen, '86'; slight heads of women numbered '3' to '7' in pen below.

Engraved in reverse, pl. 1, No. 98. The heads below perhaps as pl. 2, Nos. 112, etc., in reverse.

Hogarth, who introduces this head and (*i*) above as examples of the force of serpentine lines in the face (*Analysis*, Chapter XV), refers the reader in a note to the casts themselves 'because it is impossible to express all that I intend with sufficient accuracy, in a print of this size, whatever pains might have been taken with it; or indeed in any print were it ever so large'.

The sheet on which these two drawings are made has not been used on the other side for manuscript, and may be an insertion. It has at some time been bound up in a different position from the present, for the off-sets on Fol. 28, verso, no longer correspond in their positions to the pen heads and numbers on Fol. 29.

(*k*) AN OLD MAN'S HEAD IN A HAT (Fol. 30, verso)   Fig. 28

Pen, numbered '87' in pen.

Engraved in reverse, pl. 1, No. 106.

REPROD: *Hogarth Illustrated*, iii, p. 153.

(*l*) TWO HEADS (Fol. 44, verso)   Fig. 29

Pen over pencil on a piece of paper inserted from elsewhere, numbered '89', and '90' in pen over erasure, within pencil border. 6×9 cm.

Apparently not engraved.

REPROD: *Hogarth Illustrated*, iii, p. 153.

(*m*) TWO DRAWINGS OF THE MOUTH (Fol. 47, verso)   Fig. 30

Pen over pencil on inserted paper, numbered '91' and '92' over '51' and '52' in pen. The paper torn on the right; pencil border. $2\frac{3}{8}×2$ in. (6×5.2 cm.)

The lower figure engraved as pl. 2, No. 109. That numbered '91' related to pl. 2, No. 108.

Reproduced, *Hogarth Illustrated*, iii, p. 153.

(*n*) BUST OF A GIRL (Fol. 77, verso)   Plate 79

Pen over pencil, numbered '101' in pen.

Engraved in reverse as pl. 2, No. 121.

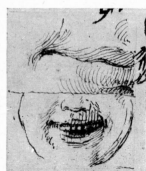

Fig. 28 (Cat. No. 81k). HOGARTH: AN OLD MAN'S HEAD IN A HAT. British Museum

Fig. 29 (Cat. No. 81l). HOGARTH: TWO HEADS. British Museum

Fig. 30 (Cat. No. 81m). HOGARTH: TWO DRAWINGS OF THE MOUTH. British Museum

82. THE OLD BABY (CRYING BOY), with other figures from the *Analysis*. *Ascribed to Hogarth.*   Fig. 31

British Museum (1858–4–17–621, L.B.28a)

Pen with brown ink. $5\frac{1}{2} \times 4\frac{7}{8}$ in. (14×12.4 cm.)
Engraved by W. J. White for Sheepshanks (B.M. Sat., 3225). For the figure of the old baby, see No. 81(e). L. Binyon is mistaken in saying that only one of the other four figures was engraved for the *Analysis*. The child and the cherub at the foot are respectively pl. 2, No. 110, and pl. 1, No. 22; the cherub at the top occurs without a number under Plate 1, No. 16. All are in the same direction as the drawing.

Fig. 31 (Cat. No. 82).   Ascribed to Hogarth: The Old Baby and other Figures.   British Museum

This drawing and three small illustrations to the *Analysis*, with a touched proof of pl. 1, were No. 757 in the George Baker Sale, 1825. They were bought by Hurst for £16 16s., according to *Anecd.* 1833, p. 398, for Sheepshanks. The three small drawings L.B. 28 (b), (c) and (d) undoubtedly belong to the second draft of the *Analysis* from which they had somehow become detached, since two of them are engraved as pl. 2, Nos. 60 and 61, and the third is an intermediate design which was not finally used as being unnecessary. While, therefore, it is possible that Hogarth as a caprice pieced together as one subject the old baby and the four cherubs, etc., shown in this drawing, the firm engraver's style is unlike that of his drawings, and it is possible that someone having obtained genuine drawings from the manuscript concocted this to place with them and thus produce a more saleable article. This suspicion would be strengthened if the anatomical drawing of a leg (L.B. 27), purchased with these by the Museum in 1858, and also in the Sheepshanks collection (*Anecd.* 1833, p. 403), which now proves to be Italian of the sixteenth century and not an unused drawing for the *Analysis* as catalogued, came from the same source. It has

a satirical bust added to it which is not part of the original drawing and may have been intended to reinforce the attribution to Hogarth.

83. LORD MELCOMBE AND LORD WINCHELSEA
Fig. 32
The Marquess of Exeter

Pen over slight pencil. The left-hand figure inscribed below 'Fig. 2 spoild' and numbered '4' above; the other inscribed below 'Fig. 1 spoild also'.
An outline repetition of the second figure and a rough indication of a gallows, both in pen, are at the foot, much torn, as are three sides of the sheet.
Approximately $5\frac{1}{4} \times 6\frac{1}{4}$ in. (13.3×15.8 cm.)

Writing on the back is visible, but it has not been possible to decipher it, as the drawing is still in the volume, where Lord Exeter has noted that it was sent to him as a present by Mrs. Hogarth in 1780. It is not included in his manuscript list.

The drawing was reproduced in facsimile by Bartolozzi, 22 December 1781, as in the collection of the Earl of Exeter. *Biogr. Anecd.* 1782, p. 323, stated that according to information given, the figures were certainly by Lord Townshend. Livesay, who had published Bartolozzi's plate, replied in 1788, in his covering notes to his *Fifteen Plates from Hogarth*, that he could not dispute the ascription to Lord Townshend, but 'the drawing the plate was done from was Hogarth's' without doubt, having been 'found among a number of manuscript notes belonging to the *Analysis of Beauty*, and the back of the paper full of Hogarth's writing'. His words are possibly an exaggeration, but there is certainly writing at the back which may belong to the *Analysis*, and the numbers and references are much in the manner of the intended illustrations to that book, while the actual drawing is completely in the style of Hogarth. The print in question, which is ascribed on good authority to Lord Townshend, is *The Recruiting Sergeant or Britannia's Happy Prospect*, 1757 (B.M. Sat., III, Pt. 2, 3581). The two figures are in the same direction as in the

Fig. 32 (Cat. No. 83).   Hogarth: Lord Melcombe and Lord Winchelsea.   The Marquess of Exeter

drawing but in the reverse order, and they are certainly very similar—that of Lord Winchelsea being closer to the caricatured form which is cut into in the drawing; but if, as appears to be the case, they were intended to illustrate the *Analysis* which was published in 1753, the borrowing would not appear to be Hogarth's.

Lord Melcombe, better known as George Bubb Doddington (1691–1762), is supposed to appear in *The Five Orders of Periwigs*, *The Election*, Plate 4, and the second *The Times*; Lord Winchelsea also in the last named (*Genuine Works*, iii, 150 *et seq.*).

84. A NUDE MALE ACADEMY FIGURE LEVERING A ROCK
                                                    Plate 25
Pierpont Morgan Library III, 32(*a*)

Red, black and white chalk on brownish grey paper, squared, incised and reddened at the back. $19\frac{3}{4} \times 16\frac{5}{8}$ in. (50.2×42.2 cm.)

COLL.: Fairfax Murray.

Recently identified, it is understood, by Dr. Edgar Wind as a drawing used for one of the soldiers in Hogarth's *Sealing the Sepulchre*, one of the side pieces of his altarpiece in St. Mary Redcliffe at Bristol (1756), engraved by I. Jenner in 1794. The identification is conclusive. In the painting, as engraved, the figure is partly draped, the head and the helmet made larger, the extreme awkwardness of the right shoulder and arm reduced, and the hands and feet differently turned; but the pose and action are exactly reproduced. Hogarth may have had an old study which proved directly adapted for the subject, if it did not actually suggest it, or he must as late as about 1756 have posed a nude model for this special purpose. Of the two alternatives, the former is the less improbable. The lever and stone would have been added to the figure which is in a conventional pose, perhaps, as suggested by Dr. L. Muenz (Antal, *Art Bulletin*, March, 1947, p. 45) modelled on one of the guards in Raphael's *Liberation of St. Peter*. For the other alternative it would be necessary to suppose that this is one of the rare cases when Hogarth, to use his own words, 'took the life for correcting the parts which I had not perfectly enough remembered' (*cf.* Introduction, p. 3), and, if Dr. Muenz's suggested derivation is accepted, that he deliberately and unnecessarily divested the prototype of his armour. Raphael's guard is fully clothed, and this would have been much more fitting in a 'Sealing the Sepulchre'. It is more likely that the derivation was indirect, through a conventionally posed model at St. Martin's Lane.

85. A SHOP-BILL FOR A COFFEE HOUSE   Plate 33
British Museum (1858–4–17–625, L.B.26*a*)

Pen and black ink over pencil. $3\frac{7}{8} \times 3\frac{7}{8}$ in. (9.8×9.8 cm.) Inscribed 'Barker's Coffe [*sic*] house' in pen on the shield, 'Shakespeares' and 'by Hogarth' in pencil below.

Acquired by the Museum in 1858 with Nos. 21 and 82 (q.v.) from a dealer, among some 1,500 drawings and prints.

Both handwriting and penwork appear to be Hogarth's, but of a later period than his engraved ornamental designs.

A design in pen and wash for the ornamental border of a trade card in the collection of Sir Robert Witt is attributed to Hogarth (with his initials) on the strength of its undoubted similarity to Hogarth's own shop card of about 1720 (reproduced as the end paper of A. Dobson's 1907 edition). That card is, however, entirely without individuality, except in the two supporting figures, and these have no counterpart in Sir Robert Witt's drawing. On the other hand, two cherubs which occur in the drawing are in a somewhat different idiom from those in the shop-card.

86. THE SLEEPING HOUSEWIFE   Fig. 33
Ascribed to Hogarth.

British Museum (G.G. 3, 66, L.B.30)

Pen with grey and brown washes, over slight pencil. $8\frac{7}{8} \times 11\frac{1}{2}$ in. (22.5×29.2 cm.)

A false signature, 'W. Hogarth', with date '1754' at foot, left; inscribed at the back (according to Laurence Binyon, in the handwriting of Mr. Eyre, a former possessor), in pencil, 'N.B. received this of T. Forrest Esq., in exchange for one of P. Sandby. Cost £9 9s.; it was given to him by Mr. Hogarth with another small scetch of a man reading'.

Stated to have been bequeathed by the Rev. C. M. Cracherode, 1799, but, as in other cases, this drawing has been included in that collection at the Museum by mistake. The inscription shows that it is the drawing mentioned by J. B. Nichols, *Anecd.* 1833, p. 399, as being in 1817 in the collection of Mr. Packer. Packer's collection was sold before 1828 to the British Museum. (*Cf.* also *Genuine Works*, iii, 274 and 288.)

This drawing is tentatively connected in *Anecd.* 1833 with the *Farmer's Return*, no doubt because the interior suggests a farmhouse. Variable as is Hogarth's style, the drawing differs from any of its manifestations in every detail, except perhaps the cat.

87. THOMAS SMITH, JONATHAN TYERS' BOOK-KEEPER AT VAUXHALL
Ascribed to Hogarth.

British Museum (1928–17–4–13)

Black chalk. $7\frac{1}{8} \times 5\frac{3}{8}$ in. (18.1×13.6 cm.)

Inscribed at the top, 'past 4 o'clock in ye morg', and on the opposite pages of an open ledger, 'Receipts on a Gala Night' and 'Vauxhall', all in a handwriting which is not recognizable as Hogarth's.

Acquired 17 April 1928 from Mrs. Percy Gye, with other material relating to Vauxhall.

There appears to be nothing in this drawing except its connection with Vauxhall to suggest an attribution to Hogarth.

88. BENJAMIN READ   Plate 86
The Marquess of Exeter

Pen and brown ink and grey wash over pencil on brownish paper, touches of red chalk. $10\frac{5}{8} \times 9\frac{3}{4}$ in. (27×24.7 cm.)

A note in Lord Exeter's hand in his book of engravings from which the drawing has been taken for mounting reads: 'Hogarth's original drawing of Mr. Ben Read given to Ld. Exeter the 21st of Nov. 1782 by Mr. Forrest'. The entry in Lord Exeter's MS. list, 1782 for this and No. 30 is: 'Original drawings of Gabriel Hunt and Ben Read from Mrs. Hogarth Nov. 21st 1782'. Livesay, in his covering note of 1788 to his facsimiles of 1781 after Hogarth, says that the two drawings now in the possession of the Earl of Exeter 'hung many years in the club-room where they were drawn, and then came into the hands of Mr. Thomas Forrest, who thinking that of whatever value they might prove to be, none was so well entitled to it as Mrs. Hogarth, presented them to her, and she transmitted them to his Lordship, who returned a genteel

suggest that this is Hogarth's own drawing, though the figure of Tristram's father is almost incredibly clumsy.

91. STUDY FOR A PORTRAIT GROUP   Plate 88
British Museum (1885–7–11–261. L.B.17)

Red chalk, pen with brown ink, grey wash and watercolour. $12\frac{3}{4} \times 17\frac{1}{4}$ in. (32.4 × 43.8 cm.)

REPROD.: A. Dobson, 1902, p. 166 (in colour).

EXHIB.: Grosvenor Gallery 1877, No. 382 (Cheney).

This drawing was acquired by the Museum in July 1885 as from the Cheney Collection, Lot 32 in the sale on 29 April 1885 (bought by Colnaghi £40). According to Laurence Binyon it was previously in the William Russell collection, but it does not bear his mark nor is it traceable in the sale catalogues of his collection (1863 and 1884). The next lot in the Cheney Sale was a sleeping child which, though not then bought for the Museum, is probably No. 92.

The paragraph regarding Dr. Lort's collection of drawings by Hogarth in *Biogr. Anecd.* 1781, p. 66, mentions together 'a coloured sketch of a family picture with ten whole-length figures most insipidly employed', and 'a head of a sleeping child, in colours, as large as life', and this is repeated in subsequent editions although all the remainder of the paragraph is eliminated. Dr. Lort's collection was dispersed in 1791 in one lot of engravings and drawings, and the survival into *Anecd.* 1833, p. 376 of the reference to these two drawings suggests that their then whereabouts was unknown at that date. The collocation in the Cheney collection and at the Museum of two drawings answering to this description may be fortuitous, or it may be due to knowledge of the reference itself, but it is also possible that they were in fact kept together, just as it is probable that both drawings came to the British Museum from the Cheney collection, although at different times and by different routes. In any case the impression of identity created by their present collocation goes further and extends to the question of authenticity; for an attribution in Dr. Lort's collection is not to be disregarded lightly. Apart from this, while the broken and shaky pen work is sufficiently in Hogarth's manner, the spineless and languorous type of insipidity is scarcely his, and the colouring and the deliberate suavity of composition are so unusual in him as to arouse more than a suspicion that the attribution, even if it goes back to Dr. Lort himself, is mistaken. If the drawing is to be regarded as Hogarth's, it must be supposed that at a late period in his life he returned to conversation pictures and in an entirely different mood from that of his early days.

92. THE HEAD OF A SLEEPING CHILD   Plate 87
British Museum (1895–12–14–1, L.B.21)

Black and red chalk on grey paper. Two corners made up. $9 \times 10\frac{7}{8}$ in. (22.9 × 27.6 cm.)

Acquired from Colnaghi in December 1895. Presumably *A Sleeping Child*, Cheney Collection, exhibited Grosvenor Gallery, 1877, No. 1016; Sale, Sotheby's, 29 April 1885, Lot 333, bought Meder £2.

For the probable history of this drawing see on No. 91.

The character of the model would give ample reason for Hogarth to make a drawing in chalk, possibly for use in a conversation piece instead of painting directly on his canvas.

Fig. 36 (Cat. No. 93).   ASCRIBED TO HOGARTH:
A LADY, SEATED.   British Museum

93. A LADY, SEATED   Fig. 36
Ascribed to Hogarth.

British Museum (1890–10–13–3, L.B.20)

Black and white chalk and stump, on buff (L.B. grey) paper. $14\frac{3}{4} \times 9\frac{7}{8}$ in. (37.5 × 25.1 cm.)

Purchased 13 October 1890 from Fairfax Murray for £1 1s.

There is no indication of the grounds on which the attribution of this drawing to Hogarth was based. Presumably the attribution was made on grounds of style, but as in the cases of the innumerable oil portraits of the period which are attributed to Hogarth in ignorance of their real authors, the argument from style alone carries no weight. With the oil paintings indeed there are genuine examples with which the pretenders can be compared. With sketch drawings of the type of the present example there is no such criterion. The portrait sketches by Hogarth which are known from early engravings, are either semi-caricatures such as the *Wilkes* (No. 95), *Ben Read* (No. 88), etc., made when he had either no wish or no opportunity to make a painting, or likenesses from life or memory of the face and features, e.g. the *Fielding* (from memory), or *Dr. Morell*. No portrait study of the present type is known to be connected with an oil portrait. Nor is it likely that Hogarth made such drawings in preparation for oil portraits. If, as appears to be the case, he painted his subject compositions straight on the canvas without preparatory sketches on paper, he may well have proceeded to portray the sitters before his eyes without any further preliminary. This is the common practice of the portrait painter, and especially likely to be followed by Hogarth, who boasted that he could take a complete likeness in three-quarters of an hour (*Biogr. Anecd.* 1782, p. 102, note), and that he never employed assistants for his draperies, etc. It was not therefore necessary for him to make drawings showing the posture and costume for the guidance of the drapery painters.

94. DESIGN FOR A NEW ORDER OF ARCHITEC-TURE, 1760   Plate 85

British Museum (1860–7–28–65, L.B.29)

Red chalk. $8\frac{7}{8} \times 15\frac{1}{8}$ in. (22.5×38.4 cm.)

A ruled pencil vertical line in the centre.

Engraved by W. Woollett, 1760, in reverse, as the frontispiece to Kirby's (Brooke-Taylor's) *Perspective of Architecture*, 1760.

REPROD.: S. Ireland, *Graphic Illustrations*, 1799, Vol. II, p. 141.

COLL.: Samuel Ireland (Sale, May 1801, second day, Lot 318, with three others, bought by Waldron £3 10s.). G. Baker (Sale, 16 June 1825, Lot 841, bought by Thane £9 9s.) Esdaile (Sale, 25 June 1840, Lot 1290, 6s.). Standly (Sale, 14 April 1845, Lot 1001, bought by Graves £4).

LIT.: *Biogr. Anecd.* 1781, p. 67*; *Anecd.* 1833, p. 398.

The print follows the drawing closely, but the book is differently placed on the knees of the coarsely-formed cherub, and is lettered on the leaves 'PALLADIO'S ARCHITECTURE' instead of 'ANDREA PALLADIO' on the fore-edge as in the drawing; there are no bands on the column, its shadow is no longer curved with the paper, one of the diagrams is altered and a block is introduced in the lower right-hand corner. Woollett has redrawn the weathercock on the temple and has managed to misplace North and South, which are not in Hogarth's drawing; there are other small variations in the foliage, etc.

The fine work in red chalk is in keeping with the heroic type of landscape which was current at this late date in Hogarth's life. The drawing was made shortly before the accession of George III, by whose command the book was published.

As Nichols points out, the idea of making new capitals from unexpected material had already been anticipated in the *Analysis*; there is no suggestion of satire or parody in this nor in the over-plump cherub and pompous landscape.

95. JOHN WILKES ESQ. 1763.   Plate 89

British Museum (1936–10–15–1)

Drawing for the engraving, in reverse, of 16 May 1763. (B.M. Sat., IV, 4050, where the authenticity of this drawing appears to be questioned.)

Pen and brown ink over pencil; incised. Torn downwards at the top and the corners made up. $14 \times 8\frac{1}{2}$ in. (35.6×21.6 cm.) The cap inscribed in pencil 'Liberty'. Two lines of pencil written below, of which 'John Wilkes Esq. drawn from the life . . .' alone is legible.

COLL.: Obtained from Mrs. Hogarth by Samuel Ireland (*Graphic Illustrations* 1794, i, 176 with reproduction). S. Ireland Sale, 1801, Lot 318, bought, according to *Genuine Works*, iii, 206, by Waldron with three others for £3 10s. Waldron Sale, King & Lochee, 9 March 1807, perhaps part of Lot 1173. Presumably George Baker Sale, Sotheby's, 16, June 1825, Lot 751, bought Hurst, £7 7s. Standly

Collection (*Anecd.* 1833, p. 400), Sale, 1845, Lot 1284, bought Graves £8 8s. Wellesley Sale, Sotheby's, 25 June, 1866, Lot 711, bought Whitehead £18. Frederick Locker (Locker-Lampson) Sale, Sotheby's, 8 July 1930, Lot 37, bought in; acquired by the Museum from Mr. Locker-Lampson, October 1936.

LIT. and REPROD.: *Graphic Illustrations*, 1794, i, 176. A. Dobson, 1907, pp. 136 and 262. B.M. Quarterly (E. Croft-Murray), XI, 3, 1937, p. 132, Plate 39.

EXHIB.: Grosvenor Gallery, 1877, No. 1088. R.I. (English Humourists), 1889, No. 3.

Hogarth is supposed to have made this drawing with a porte-crayon in Westminster Hall on 6 May 1763, marking it in afterwards at his own house with pen and ink. Having made the engraving, he is said by Samuel Ireland to have thrown the drawing into the fire where 'it would have been instantly destroyed had not Mrs. Lewis, who resided in the house, eagerly rescued it from the flames'.

As evidence of this Samuel Ireland points to the corners of the drawing which 'were all demolished'. Apart from its inherent improbability, it seems that either S. Ireland or Mrs. Lewis confused this incident with another which is more plausible. John Ireland, who mentions this story (*Hogarth Illustrated*, II, p. 471*n*) in 1791 with a reference to his namesake, gives in his third volume of seven years later (p. 292*n*) a very similar account of Mrs. Lewis saving something from the flames, but in this case the object was Basire's etching after Hogarth's memory sketch of Fielding, and Hogarth threw it on the fire thinking that it was only his own drawing. Presumably John Ireland heard this tale from Mrs. Lewis herself, from whom he obtained his copy of the etching, and even this version has become confused in the telling.

The title and numbers of the *North Briton* do not appear on the drawing, and it is to be observed that there are no buttons on either side of the coat; possibly Hogarth's attention had been drawn to the abnormality in his portrait etching of Lord Lovat (*cf.* on No. 37) with which the print of Wilkes was explicitly connected.

96. THE BRUISER, 1763   Plate 90

Royal Library (13458)

Drawing for the caricature portrait of Churchill as a bear of 1 August 1763. (B.M. Sat., 4084.)

Red and black chalk, inscriptions added in ink. $15 \times 11\frac{1}{8}$ in. (38×28.2 cm.)

The pot is inscribed 'N.B.'; the knots of the club with 'Lye 1', etc.; the money box with 'Pray remember the poor'; the books with 'Subscribers to the North Briton' and 'A new way to pay old debts', and the open book under the dog with 'an (e)pistle to W. Hogarth by C. Churchill'.

COLL.: Standly, Sale 1845, Lot 905, bought Colnaghi £1 1s. The previous lot, also bought by Colnaghi for £5 15s. 6d., a trial proof of the engraving, touched by Hogarth, is also in the Royal Collection.

This sheet is so much rubbed and damaged that it is difficult to analyse it with any certainty; it may also have been touched upon at some later date. It would seem that Hogarth, having decided to substitute the figure of a bear for his own head in the *Self-Portrait* of 1746 (fig. 37), erased that portion from the plate and took an impression in red chalk from the remaining part of it. Certainly the broken outline of the dog appears to be an impression. But some of the other red chalk seems to be of similar character, and this suggests that either the impression was taken at a later stage than a touched proof in the Royal Library, or perhaps that the drawing is an impression or tracing throughout from another. The head of a bear in the reverse direction, and the supposed head of Churchill, both in red and very faint black, suggest such an underlying tracing. The letters 'N.B.' are on the tankard, not on the club as in some examples of the print. The money-box is different in form in the print, and there carries no inscription. The books under the oval, two of which are quite different from those in the *Self-Portrait*, are differently inscribed in the drawing and the caricature print. The palette remains much as in the *Self-Portrait* and the touched proof in the Royal Collection, but the Line of Beauty (which was later removed and replaced by a political print in the caricature) is in a different position.

97. THE BATHOS, 1764

Plate 91
Royal Library (13466)

Drawing for the engraving of 3 March 1764 in reverse (B.M. Sat. 4106).
Pen with brown ink over red chalk and pencil indications; incised with stylus. Stained on the left. $10\frac{1}{8} \times 13$ in. (25.5×33.1 cm.).

COLL.: According to *Anecd.*, 1833, p. 400, sent to France by John Greenwood in 1764, and obtained thence by Standly (Sale, 1845, Lot 884, bought Colnaghi £4 4s.).
EXHIB.: Grosvenor Gallery, 1877, No. 1017; Spring Gardens (Humour Exhibition), 1925, No. 4.

The drawing is vigorous with much hatching and a somewhat clumsy, much-broken line. The differences from the print are considerable, the pose of Time's head being altered, the column on which he is resting being placed on end, the clock removed, the tower heightened, the smoke reduced, etc., etc. Phaeton on the clouds is introduced into the print, as well as the moon and a number of details in the foreground. Of the inscriptions in the drawing, that on the bell is illegible except for the words 'War' and 'God': as is that on the open book below (reduced and transferred to the opposite corner in the print), where the word 'well' seems to be written twice or three times. The burning sheet at the foot of the gallows is inscribed 'The Times' twice, the scroll held by Time 'Last Will and Testament', and on the paper at the foot of the clock is written 'Nature Banckrupt'. 'Finis' in large capitals is inscribed on the smoke. Something may have been written on the signboard of the inn, but there is nothing on the gallows-shaped post where 'World's End' is written in the print.

Fig. 37 (*cf.* on Cat. No. 96).   HOGARTH: SELF-PORTRAIT.
Touched Proof.   British Museum

APPENDIX

Selected list of drawings recorded and reproduced as by Hogarth but not at present traced. Other recorded drawings are mentioned in the introduction and catalogue. The list makes no claim to be exhaustive.

98. MODERN MILITARY PUNISHMENT, 1725. Fig. 38

Reproduced by S. Ireland (*Graphic Ill.*, I, 54) with an engraving which he attributed to J. Sympson Junr., and supposed to have been intended, with two similar prints by Hogarth, for a projected continuation of Beaver's *Roman Military Punishments* (1725), for which Hogarth had furnished fifteen headpieces. Twelve of these are said (*l.c.*) to have been reprinted.

Possibly Lot 886 in the Standly Sale, 'Roman Military Punishments, original drawing of the third plate' bought Colnaghi £1.

Fig. 38 (Cat. No. 98). AFTER HOGARTH:
MODERN MILITARY PUNISHMENT.
Etching by S. Ireland

99. BUST OF HESIOD, 1728

Engraved by Hogarth, *ex Musaeo Pembrokiano*, for Thomas Cooke's translation of Hesiod, 1728, and reproduced in *Graphic Ill.*, I, 85.
COLL.: S. Ireland Sale, 1797, Lot 128. Standly (*Anecd.*, 1833, p. 393), Sale, 1845, Lot 1050, bought Graves 5s. Capel Cure Sale, 1905, Lot 102, with another, see on No. 114 *infra*.

100. JOHN DENNIS Fig. 39

Reproduced by S. Ireland (*Graphic Ill.*, II, 78) as from a sketch, in his own possession, very slightly marked on blue paper, the pencil work below being very discernible. He concludes that it was a rapid sketch after the manner of the 'thumb-nail' drawings. It would be interesting to know whether the blue paper was that of the Sketchbook drawings (Nos. 23, etc.). Dennis died in 1734. According to Ireland, the inscription was in Hogarth's hand. This does not appear in the 'facsimile' engraving which, further, does not bear out the description of the drawing as 'slightly marked'. Quite possibly the drawing was an imposture; *cf.* on No. 89 and Introd., p. 11 *note*.
According to *Anecd.*, 1833, p. 402 (followed by A.D. 1907, p. 278), in the Royal Collection, but not, in fact, traceable there.

101. A SCENE FROM MOLIÈRE'S *MISER*, 1732. Fig. 40

Reproduced by S. Ireland, in aquatint, *Graphic Ill.*, II, 76, as the drawing in 'indian ink wash and bold pen outline with bistre' in his possession for one of two engravings by J. van der Gucht after Hogarth for the English translation of Molière, 1732. The other was a frontispiece to *Le Cocu Imaginaire*.
SALES: S. Ireland Sale, 1801, Lot 318, 'Scene in Molière with three others (Nos. 94, 95 and 106, bought Waldron £3 10s.). G. Baker Sale, 1825, Lot 749, bought Thane £12 12s. for Esdaile. Esdaile Sale, 1840, Lot 1288, bought Hodgson £4 14s. 6d. Standly Sale, 1845, Lot 1162, bought Graves £4.

102. WOMAN SWEARING A CHILD TO A GRAVE CITIZEN, 1735

According to *Anecd.*, 1833, p. 394, a pencil drawing 13¼ × 10 in., used for the engraving, in reverse, of 1735, was in the Royal Collection. There is no trace of it now. A drawing, *Swearing a Bastard Child*, was Lot 311 in the S. Ireland Sale, 1801, with the *Game at Hazard* (No. 20).
There were an oil painting and copies, both of it and the engraving. The drawing may have been made for, or from, one of these.

Fig. 39 (Cat. No. 100). JOHN DENNIS.
Etching by S. Ireland

Fig. 40 (Cat. No. 101).   After Hogarth:
A Scene from Molière's Miser.
Aquatint by S. Ireland

103. SOLSULL, A MAKER OF PUNCHES FOR ENGRAVERS   Fig. 41

Etched by S. Ireland, 1781, from a drawing in his possession (*Biogr. Anecd.*, 1781, p. 67*).
S. Ireland Sale, 1797, Lot 130, with three others not named.

104. (*a*) A SHEPHERD BOY. (*b*) A SLEEPING SHEPHERD

A soft ground etching by S. Ireland, 1786, re-issued in *Graphic Ill.*, I, p. 116, is said by him to have been 'after one of many sketches avowedly designed by Hogarth for the works of Lambert'. *A Sleeping Shepherd* in black chalk (soft ground etching by Jane Ireland) in *Graphic Ill.*, II, p. 94, perhaps also from this group, is more idyllic and even less Hogarthian in character.
A *Sketch of a Shepherd Boy* with a copy and another drawing formed Lot 132 of the S. Ireland Sale, 1797, and nine drawings, 'Various from Lambert and Hogarth', were included in his 1801 sale, Lot 306. The *Sleeping Shepherd* at the latter sale (Lot 441, among pictures, £2) would appear, from *Anecd.*, 1833, p. 368, to have been the *Female Curiosity* (*Graphic Ill.*, II, 96).

105. THE PRIZE FIGHTERS (BROUGHTON AND SLACK)

A sketch was reproduced in *Graphic Ill.*, II, p. 120, as a design (*Hogarth pinxit*) for the card of admission to the famous fight (1750) in which Slack defeated Broughton. The label is not inscribed. Nothing is said regarding the material nor the ownership and there is no corresponding item in the S. Ireland sales. A different drawing in red chalk representing this fight with 'numerous figures around' is mentioned in *Anecd.*, 1833, p. 402, as in the Col. Stanley Sale, 8 June 1832 from Udny's collection, and apparently connected with a drawing by R. Attwold, one of two once regarded as by Hogarth, and now in the British Museum. The drawing of the fight may be identical with Lot 1313 in the Standly Sale, 1845, *The Prize-fighters* in red chalk, bought for £3 3s., by Bale, and at his sale, 16 May 1881, presumably was Lot 407, 'Broughton and Slack the Prize fighters, in red chalk, from the Strawberry Hill collection', bought by Hamilton for £38 17s.

Fig. 41 (Cat. No. 103).   After Hogarth:
Solsull, A Maker of Punches for Engravers.
Etching by S. Ireland

106. SATIRE ON FALSE PERSPECTIVE, 1754. Fig. 42

Reproduced *Graphic Ill.*, II, p. 134, in aquatint by Le Coeur as the original drawing in Indian ink, given to S. Ireland by Kirby's daughter, for the engraved frontispiece, by L. Sullivan after Hogarth, to Kirby's 1754 edition of Brooke Taylor's *Perspective*. A very rough print of the 'original oil sketch' is given also (*ibid.* I, 158).

Fig. 42 (Cat. No. 106). AFTER HOGARTH:
SATIRE ON FALSE PERSPECTIVE.
Aquatint by Le Coeur

Sales: S. Ireland, 1801, Lot 318 with No. 101, *q.v.*, etc., bought by Waldron (*Anecd.*, 1833, p. 398). G. Baker, 1825, Lot 748, bought Thane £8 8s. Esdaile, 1840, Lot 1286, bought Hodgson £1 2s. Standly, 1845, Lot 1105, bought White £2 15s.

107. INVITATION TO DINNER, FROM HOGARTH TO DR. ARNOLD KING   Fig. 44

Etched by J. Cary as a vignette on the title-page of *Biographical Anecdotes*, 1782 and 1785, from a pen drawing then in the possession of Dr. Wright. Dr. King provided the scriptural texts for Hogarth's *Industry and Idleness*.

Assuming that the etching is, as claimed in the text (1785, pp. 63 and 415), a faithful representation, this design presents an excellent example of Hogarth's broken pen line.

108. CHARACTER AND CARICATURA, 1758   Fig. 45

Reproduced (by Jane Ireland) for *Graphic Ill.*, I, p. 167, from a drawing purchased by S. Ireland at the sale of Dr. Isaac Schomberg, to whom it had been given by James Towneley, a proctor in Doctor's Commons, with a letter saying that Hogarth drew it with an old and dirty pen in the kitchen of his father's house in Christ's Hospital in answer to a question regarding the difference between character and caricature. His father (also James, 1714–1778, author of *High Life below Stairs*, etc., assisted Hogarth in the *Analysis*,

Master of Merchant Taylors') gave the drawing to James Towneley, who inscribed it with the date of the event.

For Hogarth's more explicit account of the difference, see the Subscription Ticket for the prints of *Marriage à la Mode* called *Characters and Caricaturas* (1743) with the reference there made to the preface of *Joseph Andrews*. J. Ireland's version of Hogarth's own note on that print is in *Hogarth Ill.*, III, 343.

COLL.: S. Ireland 1797, Lot 133, with two sketches (unnamed) in black chalk.

109. MR. HUGGINS, 1760

The 'pencil drawing on oil paper' mentioned by *Anecd.*, 1833, p. 329 (followed by A.D., 1907, p. 215), as in the Royal Collection is a tracing, inscribed 'Hogarth pinxt, R.L. delin.', probably from the print by Major prepared for a translation of Dante. It contains the bust of Ariosto, etc., which are in the oil-painting at Adderbury and in the final but not the earlier states of the print.

110. HENRY FIELDING, 1761   Fig. 43

A 'Mr. Fielding' was included in Lot 28 of Mrs. Hogarth's Sale, 1790, among the 'Prints and Drawings'.

The 'tracing on oil paper' in the Royal Collection supposed in *Anecd.*, 1833, p. 399, to have been made by J. Basire from Hogarth's memory sketch for the frontispiece to the 1762 edition of Fielding's *Works*, may equally well have been made from a proof of that engraving without frame or ornaments which appears to have been valued highly, and was stated in *Biogr. Anecd.*, 1781, p. 131 note, to have been regarded by Hogarth as indistinguishable from his drawing. See also *Hogarth Illust.*, III, p. 292, where the proof is reproduced, and on No. 95 *supra*.

Fig. 43 (Cat. No. 110). AFTER HOGARTH:
HENRY FIELDING.
Etching by J. Basire

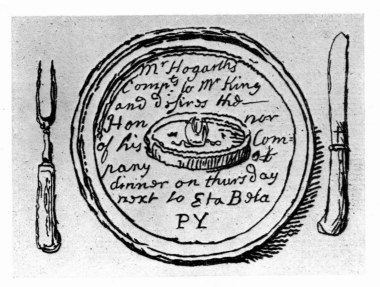

Fig. 44 (Cat. No. 107).   AFTER HOGARTH: INVITATION TO A DINNER.
Etching by J. Cary

Fig. 45 (Cat. No. 108).   AFTER HOGARTH: CHARACTER AND CARICATURA.   Etching by Jane Ireland

111. GARDELLE (by J. Richards, R.A., and Hogarth), 1761

Reproduced, in aquatint, by S. Ireland (*Graphic Ill.*, I, p. 172), as from a sketch given or lent to him by J. Richards, R.A., who made it from the murderer (an enameller from Geneva) in a cart on his way to execution, and told Ireland that Hogarth came into the room while he was drawing the portrait and added the strong touches.

A coloured proof is in the Royal Library.

112. THE FARMER'S RETURN   Fig. 46

Engraved by J. Basire as the frontispiece to the Interlude, the *Farmer's Return* by Garrick (1761). *Gen. Works*, I, p. 344,

Fig. 46 (Cat. No. 112).   AFTER HOGARTH:
THE FARMER'S RETURN.
Engraving by J. Basire

says that the original drawing was given to Garrick and was supposed to be still in the possession of his widow at Hampton (1808).

Anecd., 1833, p. 399, in a puzzling account, says that the original pen and ink drawing from which Basire engraved the print was J. Ireland's, Baker's and then Standly's, and adds that there was also a drawing of the *Farmer's Return* in the Royal Collection, 8×7 in., larger than the print. There is now no trace of such a drawing in the Royal Collection, but the title which may denote this, or No. 113 occurs in Lot 301 of the S. Ireland Sale 1801, together with a *Before* which is probably the example in the Royal Library. Standly's drawing was apparently Lot 962 in his sale 1845, bought Colnaghi £1. *Anecd.*, 1833, p. 340, specifies in this (Standly's) drawing certain features as agreeing with the first state of Basire's print but not with later states. The proofs in the Royal Library do not bear this out, but suggest that there is a con-

fusion with a close copy (in the same direction and without lettering) of Basire's print. Standly's drawing may have been drawn or traced from Basire's engraving for the purpose of the copy.

Fig. 47 (Cat. No. 113).   AFTER HOGARTH:
GARRICK IN THE FARMER'S RETURN.
Etching by S. Ireland

113. GARRICK IN THE FARMER'S RETURN   Fig. 47

S. Ireland reproduces (*Graphic Ill.*, I, p. 171) a sketch in black chalk of Garrick in this play which he describes as 'materially different from the engraved design'. *Gen. Works*, I, p. 345, followed by *Anecd.*, 1833, p. 399, speak of it as in S. Ireland's possession, and it may have formed part of Lot 301 in his 1801 sale (see above). The figure was fairly closely followed in Basire's print, and is in the same direction. A drawing described as 'Garrick in the Farmer's Return, free pen', 6¼×7 in., was Lot 716 in the Wellesley Sale, June 1866 bought by Whitehead for £12.

114. GARRICK AS THE WOUNDED SOLDIER
                                                    Fig. 48

Engraved by Richard Sawyer in 1828 as from an original sketch by Hogarth. Entitled 'Garrick as a wounded sailor' it was stated in *Anecd.*, 1833, p. 396, to be in the possession of Standly, and was, no doubt, Lot 1015 in his sale

Fig. 48 (Cat. No. 114). GARRICK AS THE WOUNDED SOLDIER.
Etching by Richard Sawyer

Fig. 49 (Cat. No. 115). AFTER HOGARTH: DR. MORELL.
Engraving by J. Basire

1845, as 'Garrick as the wounded soldier. Very spirited, in pen and india ink, from Loutherbourg, with facsimile', bought Graves 10s. 6d., and, probably, Capel Cure Sale 15 May 1905, Lot 102, Tregaskis £1 1s. To judge from the print which is in the Royal Library but not at the British Museum, the pen work appears altogether too finicky to be Hogarth's, and the one-legged figure to have no connection with Garrick. Sawyer had, in 1825, engraved a pen drawing of Garrick by Loutherbourg.

115. DR. MORELL   Fig. 49

Engraved by J. Basire, 1762, according to *Biogr. Anecd.*, 1781, p. 130, 'from a drawing returned to Mr. Hogarth'.
SALES: Mrs. Hogarth Sale, 24 April 1790, Lot 27. 'The original drawing, with variations'. Yates Sale, Sotheby's, 19 Dec. 1827, Lot 27, 'pen and ink, slightly touched with black chalk, very spirited', bought Colnaghi £4 10s., with proofs. Standly Sale, 1845, Lot 1164 (pen and ink), bought Graves £3 15s. Wellesley Sale, 1866, Lot 714, 6×7¼ in., bought Colnaghi £5 5s. Capel Cure Sale, 1905, Lot 98 with prints, bought Tregaskis £4 4s.
Dr. T. Morell (1703–1784), classical scholar, assisted Hogarth with his *Analysis of Beauty*.

116. THE BRUISER AND GIANTS IN GUILDHALL
Fig. 3 (a)

Etched (soft ground) by J. Mills, March 1817, for Vol. III, p. 163, of *Gen. Works*, as from a small memorandum book in Baker's collection, previously J. Ireland's. This book passed, with other MSS., to Standly, and after his sale into the Rowfant Library (*Cat.* 1886, p. 206, 12mo). It is now, probably, in U.S.A. The two lower figures were used in reverse for the design introduced over the palette with the Line of Beauty in the later states of Hogarth's caricature of Churchill as the *Bruiser*, 1762 (see on No. 96).

117. FOUR LOGGERHEADS, or B——E TRIUM-PHANT   Fig. 50

A small etching by White, 2×2½ in., 1818, inscribed with this title, is said in *Anecd.*, 1833, p. 315, to be from a sketch on a print of the *Bruiser*. This was probably the proof of the *Bruiser* with a sketch at the bottom in black lead by Hogarth, Lot 201 in the Ralph Willett Sale, 7 March 1814, since two other prints by White, said to be after Hogarth, *Marriage for Love* and *Rake's Progress*, are mentioned in *Anecd.*, 1833, *l.c.*, as made from drawings in that collection. No example of either print is in the Royal Library or the British Museum.

Fig. 50 (Cat. No. 117). AFTER HOGARTH: FOUR LOGGERHEADS.
Etching by White.

THE PLATES

1 (Cat. No. 2). THE LOTTERY. 1721. Royal Library

2 (Cat. No. 3).   THE SOUTH SEA BUBBLE. 1721.   Royal Library

3 (Cat. No. 12).   THE BEGGARS' OPERA BURLESQUED. 1728.   Royal Library

4 (Cat. No. 5).   HUDIBRAS: THE FRONTISPIECE. 1726.   Royal Library

5 (Cat. No. 6).   HUDIBRAS SALLYING FORTH.   Royal Library

6 (Cat. No. 7). HUDIBRAS' FIRST ADVENTURE. Royal Library

7 (Cat. No. 8). HUDIBRAS AND THE LAWYER. Royal Library

8 (Cat. No. 10).   Hudibras Encounters the Skimmington.   Royal Library

9 (Cat. No. 11).   Hudibras Encounters the Skimmington.   Royal Library

10 (Cat. No 9). HUDIBRAS: BURNING THE RUMPS AT TEMPLE BAR. Royal Library.

11 (Cat. No. 4). AN OPERA SINGER (? c. 1724). Royal Library

12 (Cat. No. 22).   Boys Peeping at Nature. 1731.   Royal Library

13 (Cat. No. 14).   A Waiter and a Hungry Customer.   British Museum

14 (Cat. No. 18). Two Pairs of Figures called 'Design for the Happy Marriage' and 'First Design for the Doctors in the Harlot's Progress'. Royal Library

15 (Cat. No. 19). 'Dr. Misaubin and Dr. Ward'. Royal Library

16 (Cat. No. 16).   DRAUGHT PLAYERS INTERRUPTED.   British Museum

17 (Cat. No. 17).   A GAME OF DRAUGHTS ENDED.   British Museum

18 (Cat. No. 15).   EXAMINING A WATCH.   British Museum

19 (Cat. No. 20).   HAZARD TABLE.   Royal Library

20 (Cat. No. 23).   Scene in the Beggars' Opera, c. 1728.   Royal Library

21 (Cat. No. 24). FALSTAFF EXAMINING HIS RECRUITS, c. 1728. Royal Library

The original sketch from the life for the principal female figure in the picture of the Pool of Bethesda at St. Bartholomew's Hospital by Wm Hogarth. This figure was drawn in St Martins lane & given to me by Tho Cotton Esq.r Nov. 21. 1794 ~ S.I

22 (Cat. No. 25).   Nude Female Academy Figure.   Before 1736.   Royal Library

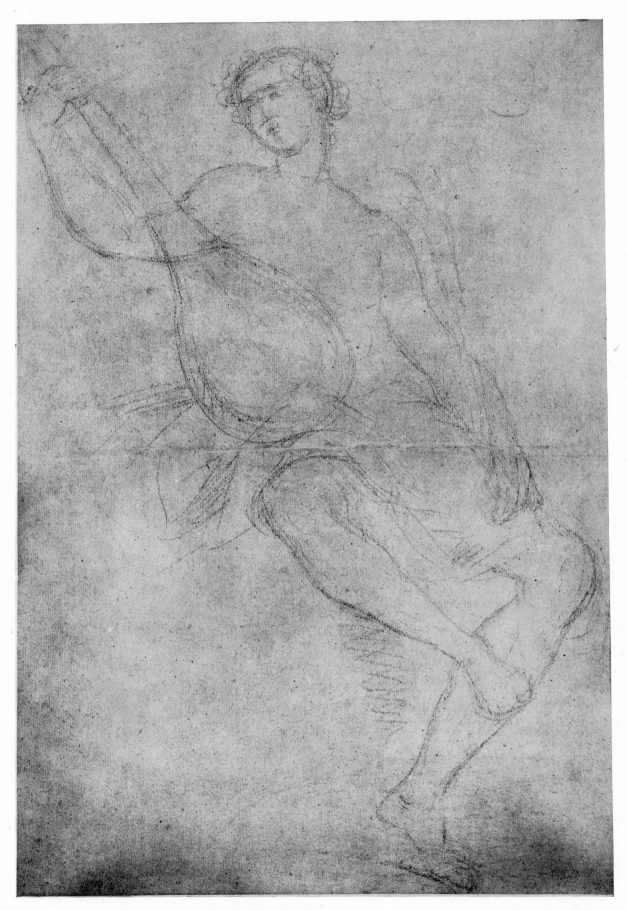

23 (Cat. No. 26).   HYMEN.   The Marquess of Exeter

24 (Cat. No. 28).   A Nude Male Academy Figure Holding a Javelin.   Royal Library

25 (Cat. No. 84).   A Nude Male Academy Figure Levering a Rock.   Pierpont Morgan Library

26 (Cat. No. 29a).   HOGARTH'S TOUR: FRONTISPIECE, 'MR. SOMEBODY', 1732.   British Museum

27 (Cat. No. 29b).   HOGARTH'S TOUR: UPNOR CASTLE.   British Museum

A. The Fisherman Shaving.
B. Mr Thornhill
C. Mr Tothall Shaving himself

D. Mr Hogarth Drawing this Drawing
E. Mr Forrest at Breakfast
F. Mr Scott Finishing a Drawing

28 (Cat. No. 29c). HOGARTH'S TOUR: BREAKFAST AT THE NAG'S HEAD. British Museum

A. The Boat
B. Mr Tothall at the Helm
C. Mr Thornhill lending a Hand to
D. Mr Hogarth

E. Mr Forrest Pushing forward
F. Mr Scott,
G. Sheerness.

29 (Cat. No. 29d). HOGARTH'S TOUR: THE EMBARKATION FOR SHEERNESS. (With Samuel Scott). British Museum

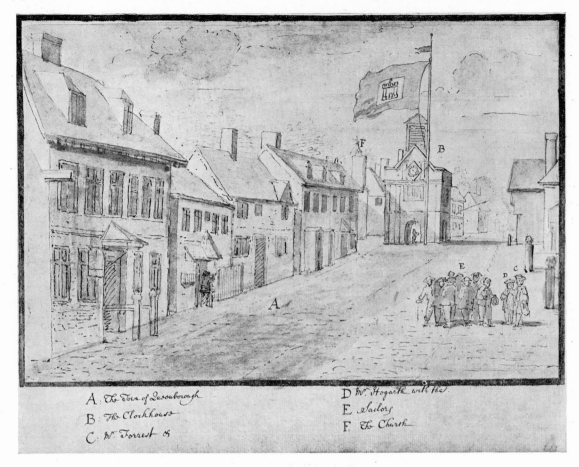

A. The Town of Queenborough
B. The Clockhouse
C. Mr. Forrest &
D. Mr. Hogarth with the
E. Sailors
F. The Church

30 (Cat. No. 29e).   HOGARTH'S TOUR: QUEENBOROUGH.   British Museum

31 (Cat. No. 29f).   HOGARTH'S TOUR: TOMB OF LORD SHORLAND IN MINSTER CHURCH.   British Museum

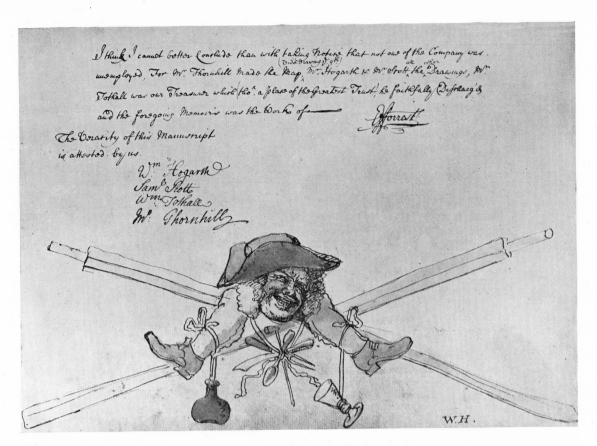

32 (Cat. No. 29g). HOGARTH'S TOUR: TAILPIECE, 'MR. NOBODY'. British Museum

33 (Cat. No. 85). A SHOP-BILL FOR A COFFEE HOUSE. British Museum

34 (Cat. No. 30).   GABRIEL HUNT, C. 1733.   The Marquess of Exeter

35 (Cat. No. 34). Don Quixote Releases the Galley-Slaves. Before 1738. Royal Library

36 (Cat. No. 36).   THE PILGRIMS AT CUMBERS. 1740.   Pierpont Morgan Library

Oct 21 1746

If the exact Figure of Mr Quin, were to be reduc'd to the size of the print of Mr Garrick it would seem to be the shortest man of the two, because Mr Garrick is of a taller proportion.
examples

a very short proportion   Quin   Garrick   a very tall proportion

Let these figures be doubled down so as to be seen but one at once, then let it be ask'd which represents the Tallest man
yours W H

37 (Cat. No. 39). THE PROPORTIONS OF GARRICK AND QUIN. 1746. Royal Library

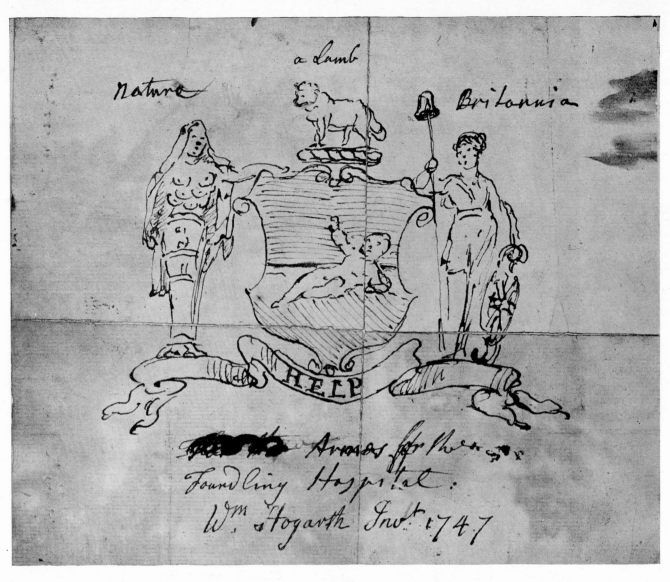

Nature

a Lamb

Britannia

HELP

Arms for the
Foundling Hospital:
Wm. Hogarth Invt. 1747

38 (Cat. No. 66).   ARMS FOR THE FOUNDLING HOSPITAL. 1747.   The Marquess of Exeter

39 (Cat. No. 78).   FAT MAN UPSET LIKE A TURTLE.   The Marquess of Exeter

40 (Cat. No. 67).   HEADPIECE TO THE JACOBITE'S JOURNAL. 1747.   Royal Library

41 (Cat. No. 40). THE FELLOW 'PRENTICES AT THEIR LOOMS. 1747. Sketch for pl. 1. British Museum

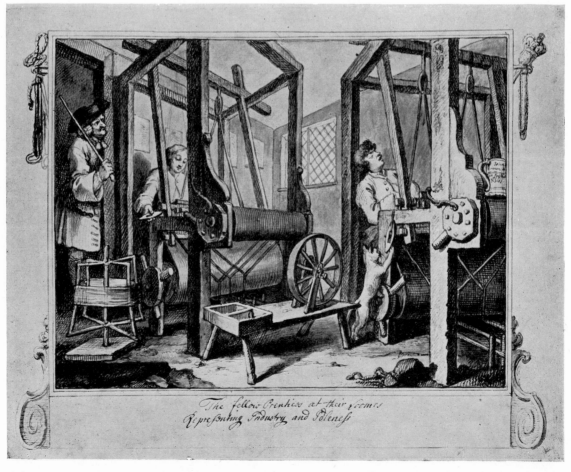

42 (Cat. No. 41). THE FELLOW 'PRENTICES AT THEIR LOOMS. Finished drawing for pl. 1. British Museum

43 (Cat. No. 42).   THE INDUSTRIOUS 'PRENTICE PERFORMING THE DUTY OF A CHRISTIAN.
Sketch for pl. 2.   British Museum

The good 'Prentice at Church Performing the Duty of a Christian

44 (Cat. No. 43).   THE INDUSTRIOUS 'PRENTICE PERFORMING THE DUTY OF A CHRISTIAN.
Finished drawing for pl. 2.   British Museum

45 (Cat. No. 44).   THE IDLE 'PRENTICE AT PLAY IN THE CHURCHYARD DURING DIVINE SERVICE.
Sketch for pl. 3.   British Museum

The bad Prentice at play in the Church yard with Pickpokets

46 (Cat. No. 45).   THE IDLE 'PRENTICE AT PLAY IN THE CHURCHYARD DURING DIVINE SERVICE.
Finished drawing for pl. 3.   British Museum

47 (Cat. No. 46). THE INDUSTRIOUS 'PRENTICE A FAVOURITE AND ENTRUSTED BY HIS MASTER.
Sketch for pl. 4. British Museum

48 (Cat. No. 47). THE INDUSTRIOUS 'PRENTICE A FAVOURITE AND ENTRUSTED BY HIS MASTER.
Final (?) drawing for pl. 4. British Museum

49 (Cat. No. 48).   THE IDLE 'PRENTICE TURNED AWAY AND SENT TO SEA.
Sketch and final (?) drawing for pl. 5.   British Museum

50 (Cat. No. 57).   THE INDUSTRIOUS 'PRENTICE MARRIED AND FURNISHING HIS HOUSE.
Not engraved.   The Marquess of Exeter

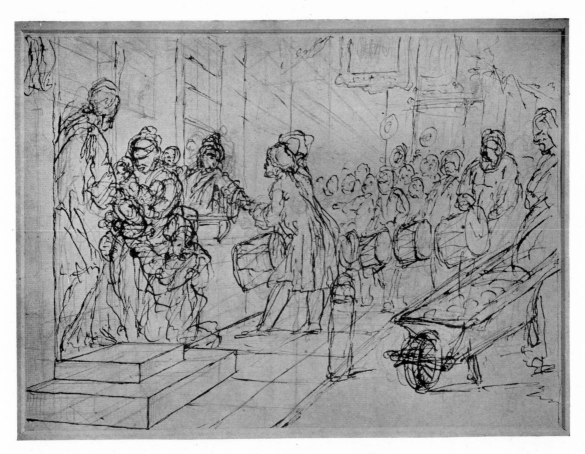

51 (Cat. No. 49).   THE INDUSTRIOUS 'PRENTICE OUT OF HIS TIME AND MARRIED TO HIS MASTER'S DAUGHTER.
Sketch for pl. 6.   The Marquess of Exeter

52 (Cat. No. 50).   THE INDUSTRIOUS 'PRENTICE OUT OF HIS TIME AND MARRIED TO HIS MASTER'S DAUGHTER.
Further sketch for pl. 6.   British Museum

53 (Cat. No. 51).   THE IDLE 'PRENTICE RETURNED FROM SEA. Sketch for pl. 7.   The Marquess of Exeter

54 (Cat. No. 52).   THE IDLE 'PRENTICE RETURNED FROM SEA. Further sketch for pl. 7.   British Museum

55 (Cat. No. 53).   THE IDLE 'PRENTICE RETURNED FROM SEA.   Advanced drawing for pl. 7.   British Museum

56 (Cat. No. 54).   THE INDUSTRIOUS 'PRENTICE GROWN RICH AND SHERIFF OF LONDON.
Sketch for pl. 8.   British Museum

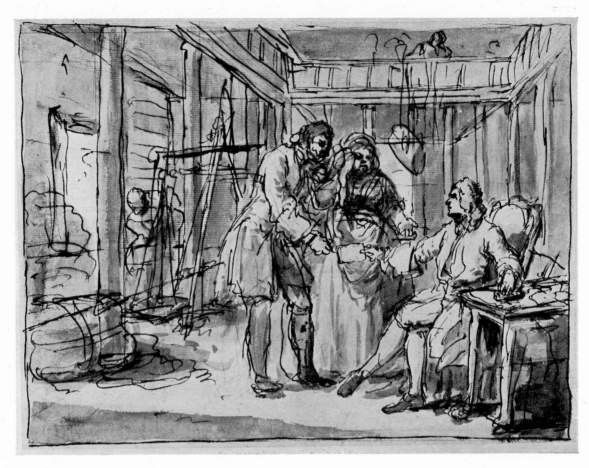

57 (Cat. No. 55). THE INDUSTRIOUS 'PRENTICE, WHEN A MERCHANT, GIVING MONEY TO HIS PARENTS. Not engraved. British Museum

58 (Cat. No. 56). THE IDLE 'PRENTICE STEALING FROM HIS MOTHER. Not engraved. British Museum

59 (Cat. No. 58). THE IDLE 'PRENTICE BETRAYED BY HIS WHORE AND TAKEN IN A NIGHT CELLAR
WITH HIS ACCOMPLICE.   Sketch for pl. 9.   British Museum

60 (Cat. No. 59).   THE IDLE 'PRENTICE BETRAYED BY HIS WHORE AND TAKEN IN A NIGHT CELLAR
WITH HIS ACCOMPLICE.   Further sketch for pl. 9.   The Marquess of Exeter

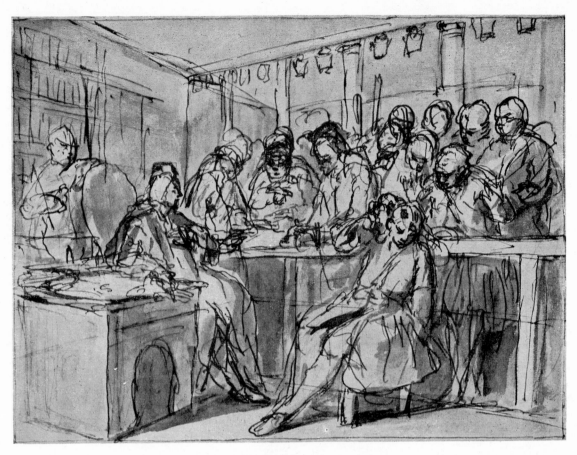

61 (Cat. No. 60). THE INDUSTRIOUS 'PRENTICE ALDERMAN OF LONDON, THE IDLE ONE BROUGHT
BEFORE HIM AND IMPEACHED BY HIS ACCOMPLICE. Sketch for pl. 10. British Museum

62 (Cat. No. 61). THE INDUSTRIOUS 'PRENTICE ALDERMAN OF LONDON, THE IDLE ONE BROUGHT BEFORE
HIM AND IMPEACHED BY HIS ACCOMPLICE. Further sketch for pl. 10. The Marquess of Exeter

63 (Cat. No. 62).   THE INDUSTRIOUS 'PRENTICE ALDERMAN OF LONDON, THE IDLE ONE BROUGHT
BEFORE HIM AND IMPEACHED BY HIS ACCOMPLICE. Finished drawing for pl. 10.   British Museum

64 (Cat. No. 63).   THE IDLE 'PRENTICE EXECUTED AT TYBURN.   Finished drawing for pl. 11. British Museum

Sketch for the Harlots Progress but never engrav'd

65 (Cat. No. 64).   AN OPERATION SCENE IN A HOSPITAL.   The Marquess of Exeter

66 (Cat. No. 65).   AN OPERATION SCENE IN A HOSPITAL.   Pierpont Morgan Library

67 (Cat. No. 70).   THE FIRST STAGE OF CRUELTY.   1750. The Marquess of Exeter

68 (Cat. No. 71).   THE FIRST STAGE OF CRUELTY.   Pierpont Morgan Library

69 (Cat. No. 72).   THE SECOND STAGE OF CRUELTY.   Pierpont Morgan Library

70 (Cat. No. 73).   THE THIRD STAGE OF CRUELTY.   Pierpont Morgan Library

71 (Cat. No. 74).   THE REWARD OF CRUELTY.   Royal Library

72 (Cat. No. 75). THE REWARD OF CRUELTY. Pierpont Morgan Library

73 (Cat. No. 76).   BEER STREET. 1750-1.   Pierpont Morgan Library

GIN STREET

74 (Cat. No. 77).   GIN LANE. 1750-1. Pierpont Morgan Library

75 (Cat. No. 79a). GEORGE TAYLOR'S EPITAPH: DEATH GIVING GEORGE TAYLOR A CROSS BUTTOCK.
c. 1750. The Marquess of Exeter

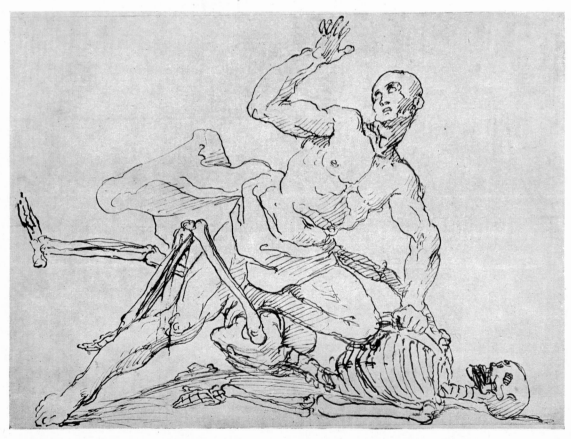

76 (Cat. No. 79b). GEORGE TAYLOR'S EPITAPH: GEORGE TAYLOR BREAKING THE RIBS OF DEATH.
c. 1750. The Marquess of Exeter

77 (Cat. No. 81e).   THE ANALYSIS OF BEAUTY: THE 'OLD BABY', THE CHILD IN A MAN'S WIG, AND
THE BALLET DANCER. British Museum

The Analysis of Beauty, 1753

78 (Cat. No. 81h). Sancho Panza (after Coypel)   79 (Cat. No. 81n).   Bust of a Girl

British Museum

80 (Cat. No. 81i).   The Analysis of Beauty: From an Antique Head.   British Museum

81 (Plate 81j).   THE ANALYSIS OF BEAUTY: AN OLD MAN'S HEAD BY FIAMMINGO. British Museum

82 (Cat. No. 81a).   THE ANALYSIS OF BEAUTY: HENRY VIII, HERCULES AND A FRENCH
DANCING-MASTER.   British Museum

83 (Cat. No. 81b).   THE ANALYSIS OF BEAUTY: LAOCOON, AN ORNAMENTAL PINEAPPLE.   British Museum

In Architecture after Filney hath been strictly and geometrically complied with, all the additional ornamental numbers of parts, may, by the foregoing rules of composing be continualy varied and yet always pleasing for example if the concave shapes of fig 2 are tolerable what may not be done with truly elegant forms as flowing shells &c

84 (Cat. No. 81g).   THE ANALYSIS OF BEAUTY: A CAPITAL
OF HATS AND PERIWIGS.   British Museum

85 (Cat. No. 94).   DESIGN FOR A NEW ORDER OF ARCHITECTURE: FRONTISPIECE TO KIRBY'S PERSPECTIVE
OF ARCHITECTURE. 1760.   British Museum

86 (Cat. No. 88).   BENJAMIN READ. C. 1757.   The Marquess of Exeter

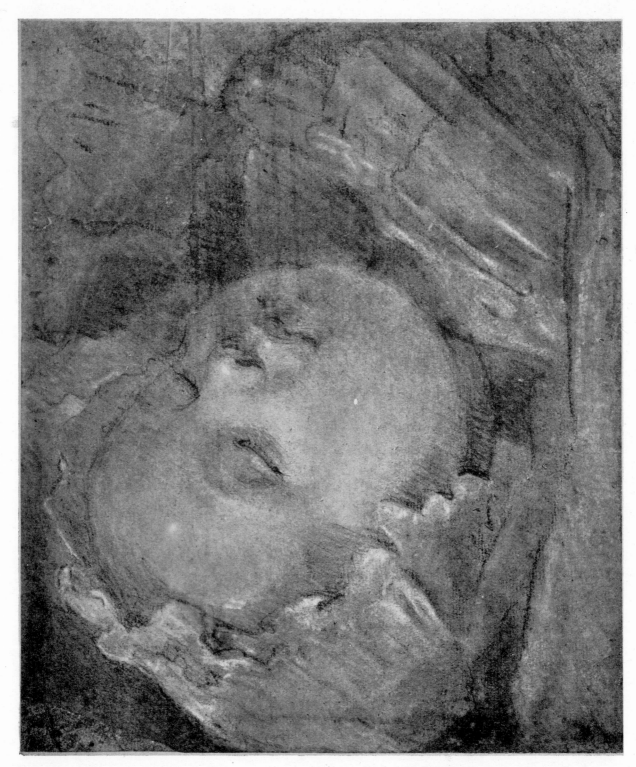

87 (Cat. No. 92). The Head of a Sleeping Child. British Museum

88 (Cat. No. 91). STUDY FOR A PORTRAIT GROUP. British Museum

89 (Cat. No. 95). JOHN WILKES, ESQ. 1763. British Museum

90 (Cat. No. 96).   THE BRUISER. 1763.   Royal Library

91 (Cat. No. 97).   THE BATHOS. 1764.   Royal Library

INDEX

Numbers *in italics* refer to pages, mainly in the Introduction.
Other numbers refer to the Catalogue, the larger figures
indicating the drawings which are catalogued in full

INDEX

INDEX